Welcome to a Destinée Media publication. Destinée aims to bring a fresh perspective to living and thinking Christianity. We thank you for your interest in our materials and hope that you find them both relevant and challenging.

At Destinée Media we seek to operate by faith in God within a Biblical/Christian worldview. We hope to inspire culture-making in creating and promoting living ideas that will contribute to Christ being understood as Lord of the whole of life, which is to be marked by redemption and renewal. We are committed to reflecting carefully on vital matters for the church and the academy, while aiming to keep a personal and intimate dimension of the Christian life in view. Destinée is interested in people and shares in several key aspects of the L'Abri ethos, including being innovative, living truth in love, and supporting the arts.

We focus on the content of our books, but also try to ask questions concerning the book as a media. One of our aims is to challenge our own perception of how a book works. Design plays a significant role: "Can a less obvious typeface help the reader to better engage with the material?" or, "Can a book cover work as a visual interpretation of Biblical themes in contemporary culture?" A clear ambition for us is to create books that connect with readers in a more human way. One surprising obstacle today is the perfection of digital typography, which might create a distance between the book and the one who reads it. How can we better communicate the humanness of the writer, designer, and reader?

We'd like to invite you to take an excursion into the theological, philosophical, and hermeneutical tension, woven into Scripture and the Christian life. Please share your thoughts on both content and book design. Do they suggest a clash of perspectives, or something of the reality of being in community with God, each other, and the world? Or Darkness, Conflict, Strength, Peace?

Let us know what you think:
www.livingspirituality.org or www.destineemedia.com

GREGORY J. LAUGHERY is the Director of Swiss L'Abri in Huémoz, Switzerland. In addition to numerous scholarly publications, he is the author of
Living Spiritual Rhythms For Today (2009),
Living Apocalypse: A Revelation Reader (2008), and
Living Spirituality: Illuminating the Path (2006).

GREGORY J. LAUGHERY

LIVING
REFLECTIONS

THEOLOGY, PHILOSOPHY, AND HERMENEUTICS

destinēe

Published by Destinée S.A., www.destinee.ch
Formatting, cover and cover bkgr by Per-Ole Lind
Cover art sample: "Una and the Lion" by Briton Rivière

ISBN: 978-0-9759082-3-5

CONTENTS

ACKNOWLEDGEMENTS

The chapters in this volume have been published elsewhere. Some have been rewritten, others I have left the same. I'm grateful to Per-Ole Lind for the fascinating cover design, and to C. Stephen Evans of Baylor University, Jamie Smith and Lee Hardy of Calvin College, Kevin Vanhoozer of Wheaton College, and Graham Mc-Farlane of the London School of Theology for taking time out of busy schedules to read and endorse this work.

Chapter one was published in Craig Bartholomew, Robin Parry, Andrew West, eds., *The Futures of Evangelicalism, Issues and Prospects,* Leicester: IVP U.K., 2003, p. 246-270 and Grand Rapids: Kregel Academic, 2004.

The author and publisher would like to thank the following for permission to reproduce material used in this book.

Chapter two first appeared in Craig Bartholomew, Colin Greene and Karl Möller, eds., *After Pentecost: Language and Biblical Interpretation,* Grand Rapids: Zondervan, 2001, p. 171-194. Published in the U.K. and Europe by Paternoster Press. Used by permission of Zondervan and the University of Gloucestershire.

Chapter three first appeared in Craig Bartholomew, C. Stephen Evans, Mary Healy, Murray Rae, eds., *"Behind" the Text: History and Biblical Interpretation,* Grand Rapids: Zondervan, 2003, p. 339-362. Published in the U.K. and Europe by Paternoster Press. Used by permission of Zondervan and the University of Gloucestershire.

Chapters four and five are moderately revised versions of material published in my Living Hermeneutics in Motion: *An Analysis and Evaluation of Paul Ricoeur's Contribution to Biblical Hermeneutics,* Lanham: University Press of America, 2002. Used by Permission of University Press of America. These pieces also appeared in the *European Journal of Theology,* VIII, 2, (1999): 145-154 and IX, 2 (2000): 159-170.

PREFACE

It is a privilege to live and work in the Swiss L'Abri community. In a day and age when Christian community is highly sought after, yet difficult to sustain, it is nothing less than remarkable that Swiss L'Abri has, through God's grace, existed for over fifty-five years. Philosopher James K. A. Smith, an occasional lecturer here comments in his book *Desiring the Kingdom* (Grand Rapids: Baker, 2009), that Swiss L'Abri is "one of the most unique and energizing environments for Christian reflection that I have ever experienced."

Living Reflections, this collection of essays before you, finds its trajectory in two key features, though there are others, of what we do at Swiss L'Abri: think critically and speak carefully about important matters for the culture, the academy, and the church. But of course, living in community is no ivory tower. Thousands of people, questioning or searching, have spent time with us hammering out a dynamic faith in the Creator and the crucified and risen One. The livability of ideas concerning theology, philosophy, and hermeneutics, or other significant disciplines, is the litmus test of their legitimacy. And tested they are, in living a life together that seeks to cultivate and promote embodying truth in love. Living truthfully and lovingly is a task, a joy, and a challenge in which God, Scripture, self, other, and the world all play a part in the drama of the unending story of creation and redemption.

One of my main interests, over the last two decades or so, has been the work of the influential hermeneutic scholar, Paul Ricoeur. He wrote, I believe, more than any other philosopher in the twentieth-century and his thought has had a profound impact in numerous disciplines, notably philosophy, theology, and hermeneutics.

This book makes its way from philosophy to parables, via the key questions of language, history, authors, readers, and texts, all subjects in which Ricoeur has made a weighty contribution. Ricoeur, therefore, is a principal interlocutor throughout the book. Each of the chapters in this volume interacts with his work, sometimes agreeing, sometimes disagreeing, with his arduous configurations, yet in both cases aiming to do so with a respectful and critical engagement of dialogue that hopefully sharpens and clarifies the crucial issues addressed in this text. There has been a massive amount of studies done on Ricoeur's philosophy, but very little on his theological trajectory and its connection to biblical hermeneutics. Situated within the modern – postmodern – interpretative debate, one of the major aims of these chapters is to ascertain if Ricoeur's richly sedimented and hermeneutically complex orientation can offer an alternative to modernist "sharp boundaries" and postmodern "radical indeterminacy." For anyone who is interested in thinking deeply about hermeneutics, language, history, the biblical text, and understanding how our own ways of reading it fit into a much wider philosophical context, I hope *Living Reflections* will be a useful guide.

In chapter one, there is an assessment of where we are philosophically today. Does Christianity in general and evangelicalism in particular, have a place for philosophy in its future? Considering its lapse of credibility on topics such as philosophy, science, and ethics, perhaps the answer is no. Yet, there are encouraging signs of renewal appearing that may be setting a course in a positive direction. Rich and creative insights are pouring forth and enhancing a critical reflection on tradition, but also making an outstanding contribution to reliable and sane ways forward for the future. Hopes for a more robust, thought provoking, and living faith are developing, especially in the field of philosophy.

Debates rage about language, which is the topic of chapter two. Postmodernism and its challenges have raised many serious questions about language and its relationship to the Bible, theology, and hermeneutics. Interacting with the pulse of these debates, seeks to bring a fresh perspective and a perceptive clarity into the conversation.

A further crucial issue has arisen through a postmodern slant. Narrative, history, and historiography are central when it comes to reading the Bible as Scripture, but the notion of history today is undergoing radical revision. Old modernist views of, "that's the way it was", are seen as duplicitous and now demand a new perspective. The rise of such a novel venture is having a profound impact on the discipline of history and how it relates to biblical interpretation, bringing forth a myriad of problematics, and chapter three attempts to engage with these.

The recent over emphasis on the reader in interpreting texts, notably the Bible, has tended to underplay the significance of the author's voice, or to exclude the author's intentions from having any significance for interpretation. Some scholars conclude that the death of the author results in the birth of the reader, which inevitably leaves textual meaning in constant flux. But the author's resurrection may still have a role to play in the interpretation of texts. Chapter four aims to explore an appropriate configuration of authors, readers, and texts, notably for biblical hermeneutics.

There is no better example of the discussion pertaining to authors, readers, and texts than the debates concerning the New Testament parables. Controversial, enigmatic, and shrewd, the parables of Jesus became the trademark for some postmodern critics to argue for a parabolic indeterminacy that functioned as a template for Jesus' mission of disorientation and negation of meaning. Parables aim to subvert, but whether they also have the capacity to meaningfully reveal is dealt with in chapter five.

1
EVANGELICALISM
AND PHILOSOPHY

Introduction

I remember the day, some years ago now, when I arrived on the doorstep of a rather large chalet, following many others to the tiny Alpine village of Huémoz, Switzerland, where L'Abri Fellowship has its home. When I got off the postal bus, after the long and arduous climb up the winding road, I met with a staff member and was welcomed into one of the L'Abri chalets for a period of study. Little did I know it then in 1980, but this day was to change the course of my life.

In the next days and weeks I discovered that L'Abri was made up of a community of people from all over the world. Each student took part in gardening, preparing meals, studying, attending prayer meetings, lectures, and discussions. All these activities, combined with the intense interaction of a community life, had the aim of being something of a demonstration of the existence of God. In addition to the centrality of Christ, a Christian worldview, a biblical spirituality and so on, one of the pivotal things that was emphasized at L'Abri, contrary to much of the evangelical focus at the time, was the relevance of philosophical ideas for understanding God, ourselves, others, the world, and the cultures in which we live. Francis Schaeffer, who with his wife Edith started L'Abri, observes:

Christians have tended to despise the concept of philosophy. This has been one of the weaknesses of evangelical, orthodox Christianity - we have been proud in despising philosophy, and we have been exceedingly proud in despising the intellect.[1]

This detachment from philosophy and the intellect did not only have harmful effects on the credibility of the evangelical community and the wider church,[2] but it left evangelicals in a dilemma as to how to interact with people, especially the younger generation, in late modernism. According to Schaeffer, the significant philosophical questions of a pluralistic culture and the worldviews it comprised were largely ignored. Unfortunately, this perspective was prevalent in many evangelical seminaries, which equally tended to marginalize philosophy. Schaeffer writes:

Our theological seminaries hardly ever relate their theology to philosophy, and specifically to current philosophy. Thus, students go out from the theological seminaries not knowing how to relate

---

1   F. A. Schaeffer, *Complete Works I*, Westchester: Crossway, 1982, 297.
2   M. A. Noll, *The Scandal of the Evangelical Mind*, Grand Rapids, Eerdmans, 1994. In this insightful work, Noll critiques Christians for similar reasons.

Christianity to the surrounding worldview. It is not that they do not know the answers. My observation is that most students graduating from our theological seminaries do not know the questions.[3]

Francis Schaeffer was convinced that Christian colleges and seminaries were short sighted here and he made every effort to broaden the vision. Christianity, Schaeffer argued, dealt with the whole of life, including the arts, music, literature, and philosophy.[4] He consistently reinforced with urgency the importance of having a grasp of the philosophical ideas that were influencing our generation and philosophy played a noteworthy role in his thought. Ronald Nash comments:

Philosophy plays a central role in the work of Francis Schaeffer. Schaeffer recognized that important developments in philosophy had helped push modern man into his present predicament. ..... It was Schaeffer's method then to look at the broad flow of philosophy and culture in the West, and to focus upon key thinkers at critical points where these problems were most apparent.[5]

3   Schaeffer, *Complete I*, 1982, 297 and see also 152.
4   Schaeffer, published books on philosophy, art, ecology, spirituality, ecclesiology, apologetics, and ethics. See, M. J. Erickson, *Postmodernizing the Faith*, Grand Rapids: Baker, 1998, 63-80, for a discussion on Schaeffer and postmodernism. See also, D. K. Naugle, *Worldview: The history of A Concept*, Grand Rapids: Eerdmans, 2002, 29-31, for a positive assessment of Schaeffer's contribution.
5   R. H. Nash, 'The Life of the Mind and the Way of Life,' in: L. T. Dennis, ed. Francis A. Schaeffer: *Portraits of a Man and His Work*, Westchester: Crossway, 1986, 53.

While Schaeffer was not a professional philosopher, he contributed to preparing the way for many who were to take up such a vocation. He discussed the works of Nietzsche, Foucault, Wittgenstein, Hegel, Kierkegaard, Sartre and other influential thinkers, when it was unthought of for Christians to do so. Though sometimes missing an astute analysis or a detailed understanding, he clearly saw the necessity for Christians to interact with philosophers and the issues they raised.[6] We owe a debt of gratitude to Schaeffer for alerting us to the significance of the mind and to the relevance of culture, but even more so, for his commitment to the Christian life that was passionately worked out in the midst of the community of L'Abri, Switzerland.

Philosophical indifference, too often an evangelical trademark, diminished the credibility of the truth of Christianity. Anti-intellectualism flourished and turned into a virtue, and it has been an uphill battle for integrity ever since. Schaeffer, among others,[7] sowed the seeds for a renewed Christian interest in philosophy,[8] which has now grown and developed in a dramatic fashion.

At present, I am a third generation staff member at Swiss L'Abri and have a published doctoral thesis on the French philosopher Paul Ricoeur. I believe, more strongly than ever, that Christians need a clear understanding of historical and

6   Schaeffer, *Complete I-V*, 1982.
7   G. H. Clark, *A Christian View of Men and Things: An Introduction to Philosophy*, Grand Rapids: Eerdmans, 1952. A. F. Holmes, *All Truth is God's Truth*, Downers Grove, IVP, 1977.
8   J. L. Walls, 'On Keeping the Faith,' in: T. V. Morris, ed. *God and the Philosophers*, Oxford: Oxford University Press, 1994, 107.

contemporary philosophical thought if they are to better evaluate their tradition and challenge their culture for the sake of Christ.

I have three aims in this chapter:

First, to provide a sketch of recent Christian involvement in philosophy, notably in North America, that gives rise to thought.

Second, to trace out three core issues that are pivotal for the present and future of the evangelical faith and philosophy:

i) the matter of the appropriate role of reason and evidence in belief in God.
ii) the debate concerning realism and anti-realism, focusing on the discussion between two philosophers: Alvin Plantinga and Merold Westphal.
iii) the problematic of the relation between theology and philosophy centering on Paul Ricoeur and Alvin Plantinga. This will be developed through a dialogue with two philosophically minded theologians, Kevin Vanhoozer and Craig Bartholomew, who creatively deal with this issue.

Third, to outline a number of trajectories for future philosophical investigation that will be pertinent for Christian thought and life.

1) The Resurgence of Christian Philosophy

An extraordinary resurgence of a Christian interest in philosophy is taking place and evangelicals are participating in this flourishing. Alvin Plantinga points out that Christians have addressed several weighty issues and contributed significantly to philosophical discussions.[9] He argues that the shining light in Christian philosophy is philosophical theology. Plantinga writes:

At present, this enterprise is faring rather well, perhaps even flourishing; the last few years have seen a remarkable flurry of activity in philosophical theology as pursued by Christian philosophers.[10]

Christian insights in philosophy and philosophical theology are having massive implications in their own right: studies on the divine attributes, God's eternity and action in the world, the argument from evil and so on, but they equally open fresh opportunities for other disciplines such as history, literature, and biblical interpretation. Evidence of this, from both the analytic and continental traditions, is found notably in the fecund work of A. C. Thiselton and Kevin Vanhoozer.[11] While Plantinga recognizes there is further work to be done in philosophical theology, positive and negative apologetics, and Christian

9   A. Plantinga, 'Christian Philosophy at the End of the *20th Century*,' in: J. F. Sennett, ed. *The Analytic Theist*, Eerdmans 1998, 328-352. See also, Noll, Scandal, 233-239.

10   Plantinga, *Analytic*, 340.

11   A. C. Thiselton, *New Horizons in Hermeneutics*, Grand Rapids: Zondervan, 1992 and K. Vanhoozer, *Is There a Meaning in this Text?*, Grand Rapids: Zondervan, 1998, whose influences include Gadamer and Ricoeur.

philosophical criticism,[12] the current renaissance of a Christian concern for philosophy is extremely positive.

A powerful stimulus for this major change has been the founding by William Alston, Robert and Marilyn Adams, Alvin Plantinga, Arthur Holmes and George Mavrodes of the Society of Christian Philosophers. Remarkably, this Society is the largest single interest group in the American Philosophical Association.[13] In addition to the Society of Christian Philosophers, one should also take note of the Evangelical Philosophical Society and its scholarly journal Philosophia Christi, renewed academic rigor, articulate published works, university postings of Christians in philosophy, and so on. These are vital signs that philosophy being done by Christians from a Christian point of view is experiencing renewed vigor in North America.[14] Nicholas Wolterstorff, Alvin Plantinga, Merold Westphal, William Alston and many others have led the way to what has now become, in a relatively short period of time, a widespread phenomenon: Christians are gaining respect for their philosophical positions and the cogency of their work calls for consideration in many philosophical debates.

This astonishing resurgence has been brought about by a diversity of factors, but analytic philosopher Alvin Plantinga has been recognized as one of its key figures.[15] In his 1983 inaugural address at the University of Notre Dame, Plantinga challenged Christians in philosophy to take the offensive and to display more integrity.

---

12   Plantinga, *Analytic*, 328-352
13   K. J. Clark, *Return to Reason*, Grand Rapids: Eerdmans, 1990, 9.
14   At present, regrettably, there are no similar movements in Britain or continental Europe.
15   Sennett, ed. *Analytic*, xiv.

Among other things, this meant embracing a greater freedom from the agendas of secular philosophy and the forging of an independence that proclaimed the right to pursue philosophical questions from within a Christian framework.[16]

Plantinga has done a tremendous amount to stem the tide of atheistic philosophy in establishing that belief in God can be rational and defensible.[17] He has also contributed significantly to the growing collapse of the argument from evil, which attempted to deny the existence of a wholly good God on the basis of the existence of evil. Christianity, Plantinga declares, is on the move, not only in philosophy, but also in a variety of areas of intellectual endeavor. Evangelicals must take notice of such a progression, and in reliance on God, make every effort to shore up the resilience and attraction that evangelicalism desperately needs if it is to hope to have a significant impact on humanity.

2) Three Core Issues

I shall now focus on three core philosophical issues that are pertinent for evangelicals to contemplate carefully. These issues are at the heart of the debate between what has frequently been referred to as modernism — postmodernism. Furthermore, each of these issues is deeply connected to the broader question of the relationship between faith and understanding.[18]

---

16   Plantinga, *Analytic*, 296-315.

17   Plantinga, *Warrant: The Current Debate*; *Warrant and Proper Function*; *Warranted Christian Belief*, Oxford: Oxford University Press, 1993, 2000.

18   P. Helm, *Faith and Understanding*, Edinburgh: Edinburgh University Press, 1997. C. S. Evans, *Faith Beyond Reason*,

i) The Role of Reason and Evidence in Belief in God

Questions concerning God's existence continue to be a "consuming passion"[19] for philosophers, and especially for philosophers of religion in the twentieth and twenty-first centuries. The role of reason and evidence in responding to these queries is a highly significant epistemological issue for evangelicals. In the wake of the audacious proclamation of Friedrich Nietzsche with regard to the death of God, can belief in God be rational?

There have been several objections raised against belief in God: the statement that "God exists" is nonsense; a lack of internal consistency in the logic that God is a personal being; the argument from evil; and that there is not enough evidence for such belief to be rational.[20] In this section, my main concern is with the latter argument: rationality and evidence.

The evidentialist objection to belief in God is that it would always be wrong to believe anything without sufficient reasons or evidence. Some evangelicals agree and contend that belief in God requires arguments, reasons, evidential proofs to be rational.[21] But others respond differently. Reformed epistemolo-

.... Dotted lines: Footnotes continued

Edinburgh: Edinburgh University Press, 1998. S. T. Davis, *God, Reason, and Theistic Proofs*, Edinburgh: Edinburgh University Press, 1997, have, in various ways, dealt with this larger question.

19   Davis, *God*, x.

20   Plantinga, *Analytic*, 102-161.

21   R. C. Sproul, J. Gerstner, and A. Lindsley, *Classical Apologetics*, Grand Rapids: Zondervan, 1984. N. Geisler, *The Philosophy of Religion*, Grand Rapids: Zondervan, 1976. In contrast, N. Mercer, 'Postmodernity and Rationality; The Final Credits or Just a Commercial Break?,' in: M. Turner, T. Lane, eds. *Mission and Meaning*, Carlisle: Paternoster, 1995, 319-338, calls for evangelicalism to shed its rationalistic-modernist framing and

gists would disagree that arguments, reason, and evidential proofs are required for belief in God to be rational.[22] As Kelly Clark points out, evangelical evidentialists have attempted to respond to the evidentialist objection by meeting its demands, while Reformed epistemology has chosen to question the credibility of such demands.[23]

In response to the evidentialist objection that belief in God requires proof to be rational, R. C. Sproul, John Gerstner and Arthur Lindsley have argued that the theistic "proofs" must not just be respectable, but if they are to be worthy of belief they must prove that God exists. "But if proofs do not prove, it is unreasonable to believe them as arguments. To do so is to say with the mind, that they do not prove and with the will that they do prove. This is usually what we call fideism rather than rationality."[24]

These writers contend that if belief in the existence of God does not measure up to the requisite standards of proof it would be irrational to believe it. They attempt to offer proof against the evidentialist objector on the foundation of evidential certainty and therefore argue that belief in God is capable of being as rational and provable as those who claim it is not.[25] In this case, the objector maintains, "not enough evidence to believe God exists, therefore if you believe you are not rational." This is challenged with the response, "of course there is plenty

become "post-evangelical." See also, D. Hilborn, *Picking Up the Pieces: Can Evangelicals Adapt to Contemporary Culture?*, London: Hodder, 1997, 56-73, for a discussion of this topic.

22   Plantinga and N. Wolterstorff, eds., *Faith and Rationality*, Notre Dame: University of Notre Dame Press, 1983.

23   Clark, *Return*, 46-54.

24   Sproul, Gerstner, and Lindsley, *Classical*, 122-123.

25   Ibid., 100.

of evidence, even proof, to believe that God exists, therefore if I believe I am rational."

It is important to recognize that these views are representative of a form of foundationalism. In the Western world, since at least the Middle Ages, foundationalism has been the central theory concerning how beliefs are to be ordered in a system of belief. A foundationalist asserts that we hold a series of basic beliefs and a series of non-basic beliefs. Non-basic beliefs require evidence if they are to be rationally accepted, while basic beliefs function as the foundation of the house of knowledge in that such beliefs are not dependent on other beliefs. But how can one be sure which beliefs are basic? In that there are various forms of foundationalism (and disagreements within them), it becomes crucial to have greater certainty that the house of knowledge is based on a solid foundation. This position is often referred to as strong foundationalism.[26] Jay Wood comments:

Strong foundationalists severely restrict what can count as basic belief, what kind of support it lends to other beliefs we hold, and the manner in which this support is communicated to non-basic beliefs. They claim that the foundations of human knowledge must be unshakably certain and that the only way this certainty is transferred to non-basic beliefs is by the ordinary logical relations of deduction and induction.[27]

---

26   J. Wood, *Epistemology: Becoming Intellectually Virtuous*, Leicester: IVP, 1998, 77-104, for a description of strong foundationalism. See also, Wolterstorff, *Reason within the Bounds of Religion*, Grand Rapids: Eerdmans, 1976, 1984, 2nd ed. for an illuminating discussion on the problems with foundationalism.
27   Wood, *Epistemology*, 85.

A strong foundationalist demands that the foundation for belief in God be certain. Basic beliefs are those that are thought to be self-evident, self-evident to the senses and unmistakable, such as, 'I am alive' or 'I am in pain,' but not 'I believe that God exists.' As belief in God here is not self-evident to the senses and unmistakable, such a belief cannot be considered properly basic, and therefore it requires rational - evidential proofs in order to justify it becoming part of the house of knowledge. If belief in God is lacking such proofs it is assumed to be irrational.

An Enlightenment notion of evidentialism or rationality has been embraced by some evangelicals who attempt to meet the criteria for belief in God that evidentialist objectors such as, W. K. Clifford, Bertrand Russell and Antony Flew, have demanded.[28] Enormous weight is placed on reason and the natural world in the attempt to prove that God exists. Peter Hicks argues:

Throughout the history of evangelicalism, there has always been a tendency among thinking evangelicals to capitulate to the demands of the Enlightenment and to seek to justify their beliefs by the use of reason.[29]

Many complex arguments or theistic proofs for God's existence have proliferated: the ontological, teleological, cosmological, and moral arguments as well as the argument from religious experience. Such a plethora of theistic proofs, however, brings with it even a fuller degree of complexity as each of these proofs or arguments

---

28   W. K. Clifford, *Lectures and Essays*, London: Macmillian, 1879. B. Russell, *Why I Am Not a Christian*, New York: Simon & Schuster, 1957. A. Flew, *The Presumption of Atheism*, London: Pemberton, 1976.
29   P. Hicks, *Evangelicals & Truth*, Leicester: IVP, 1998, 102.

is, in turn, a family of related but different arguments.[30] With this proviso in mind let us briefly consider the Kalaam version of the cosmological argument.[31] William Lane Craig proposes:

The argument is basically this: both philosophical reasoning and scientific evidence show that the universe began to exist. Anything that begins to exist must have a cause that brings it into being. So the universe must have a cause. Philosophical analysis reveals that such a cause must have several of the principal theistic attributes.[32]

One of these central theological characteristics is formulated in the following manner. If anything begins to exist it has a cause. The universe has a cause in that God created it. It is more credible to believe this than to believe that the universe came into being uncaused, out of nothing. This is a simplified version, but it legitimately represents one form of the cosmological argument.[33] In the minds of some evangelicals, if this or another type of theistic argument does not prove God's existence, it would be unreasonable to accept that God exists.[34]

---

30   For a fuller discussion of the perplexity see, Davis, *God*, and Geisler, *Philosophy*.

31   A more detailed presentation of the cosmological argument can be found in Davis, *God*, 60-77; Clark, *Return*, 17-26 and C. S. Evans, *The Philosophy of Religion*, Leicester: IVP, 1982, 50-59.

32   See W. L. Craig, *Reasonable Faith: Christian Truth and Apologetics*, Wheaton: Crossway, 1994, 77-125, esp. 92 for more detail.

33   Geisler, *Philosophy*, 190-226 and *Christian Apologetics*, Grand Rapids: Baker, 1976, 238-239, who presents this argument in bullet form.

34   Sproul, Gerstner, and Lindsley, *Classical*. See also, Geisler, *Christian*.

A second response to Enlightenment evidentialism is Reformed epistemology. Plantinga, Wolterstorff,[35] and others challenge the necessity of evidential proofs for belief in God's existence to be rational. They propose a different perspective of rationality. Nicholas Wolterstorff, for example, observes:

A person is rationally justified in believing a certain proposition which he does believe unless he has adequate reason to cease from believing it. Our beliefs are rational unless we have reason from refraining; they are not nonrational unless we have reason for believing. They are innocent until proved guilty, not guilty until proved innocent.[36]

A return to reason, in Reformed epistemology, means a refusal to let Enlightenment criteria decide what is required for belief in God to be rational.[37] This view does not attempt to meet the standards of evidentialism, but in contrast questions the legitimacy of its demands. Belief in God, it is argued, does not need evidential proof to be rational. Wolterstorff comments:

Deeply embedded in the Reformed tradition is the conviction that a person's belief that God exists may be a justified belief even though that person has not inferred that belief from others of his beliefs which provide good evidence for it. ... We have to start somewhere!

---

35   Plantinga, *Warranted*, 2000, 247-251; *Analytic*, 328-352, and Wolterstorff, *Thomas Reid and the Story of Epistemology*, Cambridge: Cambridge University Press, 2001, trace their roots back through Kuyper and Dooyeweerd to Reid and Calvin.

36   Wolterstorff, *Faith*, 163. *(Italics his)*.

37   See Clark, *Return*, 123ff. Wolterstorff, *Reason*.

And the Reformed tradition has insisted that the belief that God exists, that God is the Creator, etc., may justifiably be found there in the foundation of our system of beliefs. ... We are entitled to reason from our belief in God without having first reasoned to it.[38]

In addition to a different perspective of rationality, Reformed epistemology sets out to examine what beliefs may be considered properly basic beliefs in one's foundation. In accord with foundationalism Reformed epistemology accepts that one is rational to include basic beliefs that are self-evident, self-evident to the senses, and unmistakable in a belief structure, yet it disputes that it should only be restricted to these. Plantinga, for example, includes memory beliefs, testimony beliefs, and belief in God. These sorts of beliefs, he contends, are basic beliefs in that they are not dependent on reason, evidence or other beliefs.[39]

Plantinga and Wolterstorff, along with C. Stephen Evans, Kelly James Clark, and Stephen Davis have produced insightful and detailed work on the problematics raised in this section.[40] Reformed epistemology with its different definition of rationality and its refiguring of the notion of properly basic beliefs is funding much of the epistemological discussion today. In this view, it is not wrong to attempt to give reasons or evidence for belief in the existence of God, but these are not

38   Wolterstorff, 'Is Reason Enough?,' in: R. D. Gevitt and B. Sweetman, eds. *Contemporary Perspectives on Religious Epistemology*, 1992, 149. *(Italics his)*.

39   Plantinga, *Analytic*, 102-161.

40   Plantinga, *Warranted*, 2000; Wolterstorff, *Reason*; Evans, *Philosophy*; and *Faith*, 1998; Clark, *Return*, Davis, *God*.

necessary for one's belief in God to be considered rational. There is no interest in attempting to prove God's existence on the basis of reason or evidence, yet those who hold this epistemology forcefully maintain that God exists and that belief in God is rational.

The question of belief in God and the role of reason and evidence in such belief remain acute matters for philosophical investigation in our times. Have evangelicals too often drunk from the intoxicating well of the Enlightenment? If Enlightenment criteria and assumptions are now fading or have failed, it may indeed be the moment for evangelicals to reassess their epistemology. In contrast to a succession of barricades, which too often characterize our evangelical heritage, the aim of reassessment should be serious dialogue with the hope of coming to fecund conclusions for the Christian faith.

ii) Realism versus Anti-Realism

As Plantinga has noted, this is an important issue for Christians in philosophy.[41] Realism and anti-realism are philosophical positions directly connected to the understanding and shaping of one's world-view. When we make a statement about the world are we speaking of the real world outside of us or merely using language to construct a world, which is dependent on human interaction?[42] This controversy is clearly linked to other domains of inquiry, such as metaphysics, epistemology and lan-

---

41   Plantinga, *Analytic*, 328-352.

42   J. A. Kirk and K. Vanhoozer, *To Stake A Claim: Mission and the Western Crisis of Knowledge*, New York: Orbis, 1999, 18-34, have an excellent discussion of the realism / anti-realism debate.

guage, but my aim is to present this philosophical issue in the context of the question of our relation to the world.

Immanuel Kant, a prolific philosopher of the modern period, may still be one of the most influential and thought provoking participants in this discussion.[43] The philosophy of Kant is extremely complex, yet I believe it is possible to draw some basic conclusions that pertain to this issue. Kant is seen by some, as attempting to have the best or the worst as the case may be, of two worlds. That is, by the time of Kant, the empiricism of David Hume had brought a significant challenge to a rationalist approach, and through Hume's trajectory, Kant was awakened to what he envisioned as new possibilities for philosophy.[44] This jolt is referred to by Kant as a Copernican Revolution. What was it? Basically, Kant found himself in agreement with the rationalist notion that knowledge related to concepts formed by the mind, while at the same time he held that knowledge came from the senses.

What does this have to do with the question of the world and our access to it? Kant, as some propose, divided the world in two: the noumenal, which is the realm of things in themselves and the phenomenal, which is the world as we experience it in terms of categories we impose on it. The latter world is the world we are restricted to having knowledge about. J. Andrew Kirk puts it this way:

---

43   I. Kant, *Critique of Pure Reason*, trans. N. K. Smith, New York: St. Martin's Press, 1929.
44   See R. Scruton, *Kant*, Oxford: Oxford University Press, 1982, for a helpful introduction to Kant.

The dilemma began when the culture in general accepted (following the arguments of Hume and Kant) that intellectual probity necessitated the assumption that the uniformity of natural causes required a closed-order universe. The dilemma is acute. No longer is there a sufficient reason for believing with certainty that anything exists, or that there is an adequate correlation between the observer (subject) and the thing observed (object)... [45]

The radical post-Kantian question, highlighted by many a postmodernist is the following: can one access the world as it is? As Kirk has pointed out above, there is a dilemma with regard to the object / subject interface. Christian philosophers continue to wrestle with these Kantian or reality types of questions. I shall briefly examine two responses to Kant. Alvin Plantinga, the analytic philosopher, claims that Kant's idea of creative anti-realism in the first *Critique* is "incompatible with Christianity."[46] A realist perspective assumes that our access to the world must conform to objects and not vice-versa. Plantinga points out:

But the fundamental *thrust* of Kant's self-styled Copernican Revolution is that things in the world owe their basic structure and perhaps their very existence to the noetic activity of our minds.[47]

Plantinga is highly suspect of anything profitable coming from the Kantian notion of creative anti-realism. He seems to argue

45   Kirk, *To Stake*, 170.
46   Plantinga, *Analytic*, 331
47   Plantinga, 'The Twin Pillars of Christian Scholarship,' in: *Seeking Understanding: The Stob Lectures 1986-1988*, Grand Rapids: Eerdmans, 2001, 129, *(Italics his)*.

that we either perceive the world as it is, or that we create it as it appears, and if the latter is the case, there is no connection between the noumenal and the phenomenal. On this second scenario of creating the world, the result would be that the things in the world owe their existence to the subject. Plantinga's interface of object and subject suggests there is only one world, that is, the world that the subject sees, is the world as it is.

On the other hand, Merold Westphal, who is a more continental type of philosopher, argues that creative anti-realism is to be defended and that Christian philosophers should be favorably inclined to Kantian idealism.[48] Westphal suggests that Plantinga may have under-read Kant, arguing that there are "four types of Kantianism"[49] only one of which contains a negative humanist orientation which would be pejorative for a Christian point of view.

In his discussion of Kant, Westphal uses the example of the difference between watching a black and white TV and seeing the real color of something in the TV studio. He wishes to make the point that Kant sees the mind as a "receiving apparatus" whose "spontaneity" allows things to appear in a particular way, whether they are this way or not. This, in Westphal's view, should not be understood as two worlds, but rather as two modes of a subject seeing the same object. If this is the case, the object remains what it is even though the receiving apparatus may modify it and Kant's position, Westphal argues, is more closely represented by this type of realism.[50]

---

48   M. Westphal, *Suspicion and Faith: The Religious Uses of Modern Atheism*, Grand Rapids: Eerdmans, 1993, 162.
49   Ibid., 163, for the detailed argument.
50   Ibid., 166.

How are we to understand these two Christian responses to Kant? What type of people are human beings and what sort of world is it that we live in? These questions are at the heart of the Christian faith. Plantinga seems to make the relation between the world and our access to it exactly the same, while Westphal aims to defend the distinction. That is, he is more concerned with our "receiving apparatus" which may in fact, he contends, not receive things exactly the same way they actually are in the world.

Both these views concerning this arduous question, from a Christian perspective, seem to have valid points. Thus, I suggest the appropriateness of a configuration which respects both the relation and the distinction of the object/subject interface. There is indeed a complexity in tension that cannot be resolved by opting for either relation or distinction alone. Furthermore, it may be an opportune time for evangelicals in philosophy to acknowledge, to a greater degree, a place for human subjectivity with respect to the object/subject relation and distinction, without however, capitulating to modes of subjectivity that seek to remove or deny any objectivity whatsoever.

In my view, evangelicals who work in philosophy cannot ignore Kant and are obliged to further interact with his work, especially the *Critique of Pure Reason*. This is not to say that one must be overly pre-occupied with Kant, but only to argue that this crucial debate needs further illumination if we are to come to increasingly fecund and clearer conclusions. A greater precision in the understanding of whether we are talking about reality or knowledge, or both, and what we mean when we use the terms realism and creative anti-realism will prove, I believe, profoundly useful for a Christian understanding of God, self, and world.

iii) Philosophy versus Theology

The relationship between philosophy and theology has long been a debated issue. How are we to configure this relation? This is a massive and complex question, impossible to do full justice to here, yet it is important to bring some elements of a response into light. I shall first explore the views of two contemporary philosophers: Paul Ricoeur[51] and Alvin Plantinga.[52] Ricoeur and Plantinga are post-modern: both are aware, in their own ways, of the pitfalls of classical strong foundationalism. These philosophers, Plantinga the evangelical, and Ricoeur not, both merit a close reading.[53] Evangelicals in philosophy, or theology for that matter, have much to learn from them as they each offer, in the twilight of modernism,[54] something of a way forward to a truly post-modern philosophy. Plantinga and Ricoeur are opposed to any notion of a Cartesian self-authenticating self and steer clear of modernist forms of postmodernism. Ricoeur has been extremely sensitive about meshing

---

51   See G. J. Laughery, *Living Hermeneutics In Motion: An Analysis and Evaluation of Paul Ricoeur's Contribution to Biblical Hermeneutics*, Lanham: University Press of America, 2002, for a full account of Ricoeur's work on biblical hermeneutics in the context of modernism and postmodernism.

52   Noll, *Scandal*, 235, points out the radical resurgence of an evangelical interest in philosophy in North America is largely due to the fecund influence of those connected to the Dutch reformed heritage. Two of the leading contributors to this renewal are A. Plantinga and N. Wolterstorff.

53   Recent works by Plantinga include *Warrant*, 1993, 2000. Ricoeur, *Temps et récit*, 3 tomes, Paris: Seuil, 1983-1985, *Time and Narrative*, 3 volumes, trans. D. Pellauer and K. McLaughlin, vol 1&2, - K. Blamey and D. Pellauer, vol 3, Chicago: University of Chicago Press, 1984-1987.

54   G. Green, *Theology, Hermeneutics and Imagination*, Cambridge: Cambridge University Press, 2000, 25.

together his philosophical work and his theological beliefs and understandings, although he readily admits some effects of the latter on the former.[55] Plantinga is much less cautious in this area and deliberately acknowledges Christian presuppositions as classifying and influencing his philosophical work. Plantinga, the philosopher of religion, attempts to relate theology to philosophy, and dares to articulate a Christian philosophy, whereas Ricoeur, the philosopher, strives to keep the two distinct and would be reluctant to embrace any notion of *Christian* philosophy, as for him, this would amount to something like a round square.[56]

Plantinga lacks no zeal, and rightly so, in reminding Christian philosophers that they need not be favorably disposed to non-believing philosophies and that theologians and biblical scholars should not see themselves as indebted to the ideas and projects of unbelievers. Plantinga's work has clearly had a tremendous influence on philosophers and the philosophy of religion, especially in North America. The resurgence of philosophical inquiry in the evangelical and wider Christian community is to be applauded and Plantinga is to be given due credit for his outstanding contribution in making this venture philosophically credible and convincing.[57]

Ricoeur is heralded as one of the most important and versatile philosophers of the twentieth century. He attempts to

---

55   Ricoeur, *Soi-même comme un autre*, Paris: Seuil, 1990, *Oneself as Another*, trans. K. Blamey, Chicago: University of Chicago Press, 1992, 24.

56   Ibid., 39-40.

57   See section 1, 'The Resurgence of Christian Philosophy' above.

avoid the accusation of crypto-theologizing[58] his philosophical work, yet his hermeneutically centered philosophy is theologically sensitive. Ricoeur's notion of philosophy is that it is basically anthropology. In his perspective there is a difference between solving a question posed and responding to a call.[59] One may speak of law, conscience, guilt and so on in philosophy, although in Ricoeur's view, neither love nor the confession of sin for example, are philosophical ways of speaking as both go beyond the limits of philosophical inquiry.

How shall we evaluate the views of these two philosophers? Ricoeur seems to begin with philosophy, recognize its limits and then turns to theology. Does he leave the two too far apart? Plantinga, on the other hand, seems to begin with theology, and from this, work out his philosophy.[60] Does he too quickly integrate the two? The questions concerning Ricoeur's distance and Plantinga's integration are not intended to be rhetorical, but inquisitive.

Keeping these questions in mind, I shall now examine the perspective of two theologians, Kevin Vanhoozer and Craig Bartholomew, who are both well attuned to the importance of philosophy. In his recent treatment of the subject, Bartholomew is concerned with the question of whether current formulations of theological hermeneutics have sufficiently taken philosophy into account.[61] While he *affirms* these new

---

58   Ricoeur, *Soi, Oneself*, translation, 1992, 24.
59   Ibid., 23-25 and *Talking Liberties*, London: Channel 4 Tele., 1992, 39.
60   Plantinga, *Analytic*, 146-147, suggests following Reformed thinkers and starting with God.
61   C. G. Bartholomew, 'Uncharted Waters: Philosophy, Theology and the Crisis in Biblical Interpretation,' in: Bartholomew, C.

formulations in their theological orientation, the pressing *question* of the relationship between philosophy and theology remains. I concur with Bartholomew's endorsement and with his query.

The complexity of this issue has also been explored by Kevin Vanhoozer.[62] In putting forward what he terms a Chalcedonian view of the relationship, Vanhoozer argues for the individual integrity, the relative autonomy and the mutual accountability of philosophy and theology. Bartholomew, in dialogue with Vanhoozer, grants that precision on this problematic is difficult, but he remains cautious about Vanhoozer's framing of Christ (theology) and concept (philosophy). The concern, for Bartholomew, is that there seems to be a residue of the modernist distinction between philosophy and theology that is "somewhat restlessly present throughout" Vanhoozer's point of view, although Vanhoozer is careful to relate the two.[63]

· · · · · · · · · · ·

Greene, K. Möller, eds. Renewing Biblical Interpretation, Grand Rapids: Zondervan, 2000, 1-39, presents this in a concise and fecund manner.

62   Vanhoozer, 'Christ and Concept: Doing Theology and The "Ministry" of Philosophy,' in: T. E. McComiskey and J. D. Woodbridge, eds. Doing Theology in Today's World, Grand Rapids: Zondervan, 1991, 99-145.

63   Bartholomew, 'Uncharted,' 1-39, esp. 31. In my reading of Vanhoozer's proposal he is careful to attempt to address both the 'distinctness' and 'relatedness' of theology and philosophy.

Bartholomew proposes an intriguing and valuable modified typology for elucidating the relationship between philosophy and theology. His query, with some formulations of theological hermeneutics, seems to be the unwitting or deliberate emphasis on keeping the two apart. Bartholomew's useful typology, which he readily admits is tentative, aims to integrate the two through an appeal to Christ as the *clue* to philosophy and theology. A Christian hermeneutic, he argues, is to be viewed as faith seeking understanding in both spheres of research.[64]

This proposal points us in a helpful direction, yet my concern is whether it relates theology and philosophy in such a manner that leaves little room to continue to *really* view them as distinct.[65] If Christ is the *clue* to philosophy, how does philosophy remain distinct from theology?[66] The suggestion that Vanhoozer has been modernist in leaving philosophy and theology too distinct is countered by Bartholomew in more expressly relating the two. Does this proposal equally result in a modernist configuration in that it moves awfully close to dis-

---

64 We have no space here to enter into the fascinating and crucially important debate concerning faith seeking understanding. Where do we really begin? See section 3 'Trajectories for the future' below.

65 Bartholomew refers to Milbank, 'Knowledge,' in: J. Milbank, C. Pickstock, and G. Ward, eds. *Radical Orthodoxy: a new theology*, London: Routledge, 1999, 23-24. See also Milbank, 32 and footnote 49, which offer another argument along these lines. He points out that philosophy cannot give an account of being human on its own. "Theology *can* evaluate philosophy." While this is true, I would wager the reverse may also, at least in some contexts, have a role: Philosophy can also evaluate theology.

66 Following Newbigin, Bartholomew, (2000: 33-34) writes that Christ is the clue to all creation. In my view, theologically, the Triune God, Father, Son and Spirit, is its clue.

solving a tension through seeing philosophy and theology as too related? If this is the case, Bartholomew's point of view seeks to perhaps resolve a tension of relation and distinction that should be embraced and left intact.

The principal difference between Bartholomew and Vanhoozer can be summed up in the following way. Bartholomew's theological orientation of relating philosophy and theology seems to promote an interaction with philosophy for the purpose of assessing its negative impact on theology. He rightly wants theology to be better able to critique anti-Christian philosophies, but to do so theology has to be more aware of how it may be pejoratively influenced by such points of view. Vanhoozer's relation and distinction of philosophy and theology on the other hand, seems willing not only to assess a potential negative impact, but also to rightly affirm the possibility that philosophy might make a positive contribution to and offer a critique of theology.[67]

My main concerns are the following. If these two disciplines are too related is there a real possibility for one to offer the other a contribution or critique? Does relating philosophy and theology together too rapidly, in an unrestricted union, suggest a modernist underplay of a dialogue in tension? Should our aim be to preserve a place for philosophy to assert a relative autonomy for the sake of offering an affirmation / critique to theology, while at the same time to equally hold on to theology's task of providing the same for philosophy?

---

67   This may be closer to Bartholomew's (2000: 32) notion of "double truth" where, I would say, *different* not always conflicting views "sit in uneasy tension."

In conclusion, I would argue that as we move into the future, evangelicals should aim to avoid unnecessary polarizations (realism and anti-realism; philosophy and theology) where they are not called for. This is not, in general, to propose a form of synthesis, nor to discount that some key issues will rightly remain in opposition, but only to suggest that discovering a relation and distinction perspective on some issues, in acknowledging a tension-filled alliance,[68] may bring us closer to Christian truth.

3) Trajectories for the future

Any attempt to sketch out lines for the future may prove problematic, yet it is necessary for Christian philosophers to be aware of a number of topics that require attention. Several other issues, in addition to those already addressed, may prove worthwhile to investigate.

Plantinga has given us an excellent overview of the current state and future concerns of Christian philosophy.[69] His assessment is that Christian philosophers have done fairly well in a variety of areas, but that there is more work to be done. Pluralism, in Plantinga's opinion, will be a major question that must be addressed. He also posits that there are a diversity of positive arguments for the Christian position that should be developed and that theistic arguments are in need of greater development. Other concerns would be a vibrant cultural criticism, and a deepening philosophical theology, where major Christian doctrines are examined and better understood for the Christian community.

---

68   Evans, *Philosophy*, 25.
69   Plantinga, *Analytic*, 328-352.

Plantinga has also declared that perennial naturalism and creative anti-realism are the "hydra heads" that have arisen in the wake of the demise of logical positivism. He argues that each is pervasive in its own way, and it is essential for Christian philosophers to pay close attention as to how they infiltrate Christian thought in negative ways.[70]

In addition to the issues mentioned by Plantinga, others may also be relevant and merit further reflection. The philosophy of language remains an important subject. There has been some, but not enough work done here. Wolterstorff,[71] Thiselton,[72] and others[73] have explored the potential of speech act theory and produced excellent contributions. As the residues of positivism fade and postmodern queries proliferate, Christians have a new opportunity to join in and contribute to, a theory of language.[74]

In light of the collapsing foundations of modernism the role of communicating the gospel may become more acutely significant. What are Christian modes of communication in a postmodern world? How might philosophers help in moving us from the more abstract to insightful and practical ways of communicating the truth of the Christian worldview? A practical philosophy, not only related to thinking but living, is essential.

---

70   Ibid., 328-335.

71   Wolterstorff, *Divine Discourse: Philosophical Reflections on the Claim that God Speaks*, Cambridge: Cambridge University Press, 1995.

72   Thiselton, *New Horizons*.

73   See also, Vanhoozer, *Is There A Meaning?*

74   Bartholomew, Greene, and Möller, eds. *After Pentecost: Language and Biblical Interpretation*, Grand Rapids: Zondervan, 2001.

A pertinent question, closely connected to our three core issues above, is the relationship between faith and understanding. Faith seeking understanding and understanding seeking faith? Philosopher Paul Helm has recently investigated this relationship and made a fine contribution to moving us further along.[75] Where, when and how do we begin? In my view, this pivotal issue deserves more reflection. The statement, 'faith seeking understanding' seems to be frequently cited in Christian contexts, but not always with a great deal of focus and clarity.

Another problematic deserves further research. Since at least the era of Augustine, the issue concerning God and time has produced a diversity of questions. How are God and time to be thought of? Are we to think of God as outside time, in time, or both at the same time? What is time? Who is God in connection to time? These types of questions have begun to draw more widespread consideration. Ricoeur has produced a fascinating and insightful study on temporality and narrative.[76] He has also argued that if we are going to understand something of time and of God, it is essential to examine the biblical text in its narrative and other forms.[77] Evangelicals can certainly benefit from Ricoeur's investigations. Other recent work has much to commend it,[78] but there is more that could be done to address these questions.

---

75   Helm, *Faith*.
76   Ricoeur, *Temps et récit*, 1983-1985: trans. *Time and Narrative*, 1984-1987.
77   Ricoeur, 'Temps biblique,' *Archivio Filosofia* 53, (1985), 29-35. "Biblical Time," in: *Figuring the Sacred: Religion, Narrative and Imagination*, trans. D. Pellauer, M.I. Wallace, ed. Minneapolis: Fortress, 1995, 167-180.
78   G. E. Ganssle, ed. *God & Time*, Downers Grove: IVP, 2001.

The philosophical issues mentioned here, along with others, merit hard and careful thought. If evangelicals in philosophy are to continue on the road towards credibility, there is a crucial need to face the many challenges ahead. In order to participate in the hope of renewing a thirst for the living God and a living spirituality that touches the whole of life, Christian philosophers must not only track their culture, but also trace it. This means it is essential to be aware of the personal and cultural impact of philosophical ideas, and to leave, through an involvement with culture, a Christian imprint. My hope is that such efforts, dedicated to God and the Christian community, will challenge others to take notice that the God of Scripture is there and that Christianity is true.

2

LANGUAGE
AT THE FRONTIERS
OF LANGUAGE

Introduction

Scripture is a literary text made up of a diversity of genres and language uses. As a result, biblical interpreters have quite rightly worked with and been influenced by, various theories of language. However, in view of the skepticism implicit in some of these theories, uncritical acceptance may result in unwarranted suspicion concerning the capacity of Scripture to communicate truths about God, the world, and the self. What perspectives on language theory are to be considered useful or dangerous for the faithful art and act of biblical interpretation? How might Christians respond to the driving polemics attached to the current intrigue and infatuation with language? These exceedingly pertinent questions require the careful attention of Christian scholarship should it wish to learn from, but also eschew the perils of, the medley of language theories on offer.

In the contemporary arena of debates about language, one is faced with a puzzling question: what is a theory of language?

Is it even a possibility, without recourse to a horizon past its own boundary? How is one to talk about language in a post-Pentecost, post-structuralist, post-modern, and now allegedly post-Christian[1] world?

According to one commentator, language is a sort of labyrinth playfully deferring meaning,[2] while another argues it is a series of signs which refer only to themselves, eventually leading to an endless erring?[3] 'Meaningless, Meaningless, Everything is Meaningless' reads one translation of the words from the famous work of Ecclesiastes.[4] Perhaps, 'Language, Language, Everything is Meaningless Language' resonates an up-to-date echo of this age old commentary. All language is considered

---

1   D. Cupitt, 'post-Christianity,' in: P. Heelas, ed. Religion, *Modernity and Postmodernity*, Oxford: Blackwell, 1998, 218-232, argues that post-Christianity means: there is no longer capital - T truth, existence is in flux, human expression is our redemption, and there is only the stream of language-formed events. It is crucial to understand that Cupitt has not only embraced a theory of language here, but he is advocating a particular world-view in connection with it.

2   J. D. Crossan, 'A Metamodel for Polyvalent Narration,' *Semeia* 9 (1977), 105-147.

3   M. C. Taylor, Erring, *A Postmodern A/Theology*, Chicago: University of Chicago Press, 1984, 3, marks Nietzsche as being one of the major prophets of postmodernism with his declaration: 'God remains dead. And we have killed him.' See also, 134-135. The death of God, from Taylor's point of view, "marks the loss of a stable center" which was believed to be the support for individuality and a transcendent selfhood. "This mortal wounding of the original subject releases the erring of scripture that entwines all things." In Taylor's perspective, language "as a ceaseless play of interrelated differences" undermines the possibility of any original subject outside of language.

4   NIV, (Eccl. 1:2). This is not the end of the story in Ecclesiastes; in contrast to what some suppose is the case in the contemporary context.

suspect and void of meaning. Such a plot may well describe the current state of language theory and what has been referred to as the linguistic turn[5] in philosophy, literature, theology, and hermeneutics.[6]

The subject of language has undergone intense investigation and become a central topic of debate within each of the disciplines mentioned above. Language has been understood to be ordinary, scientific, or religious. It has also been suggested that language is language, and is grounded in nothing other than language.[7] Further claims include: language is God,[8] a gift of God,[9] and that language is man.[10] Questions of the origin, essence, and function of language have come under piercing examination and a raging discussion has ensued, which has led to a variety of perspectives and conclusions that have had an impact on biblical interpretation.[11]

---

5   D. Stiver, *The Philosophy of Religious Language: Sign, Symbol, & Story*, Oxford: Blackwell, 1996, 4-7.

6   J. Fodor, *Christian Hermeneutics: Paul Ricoeur and the Refiguring of Theology*, Oxford: Oxford University Press, 1995, 147.

7   M. Heidegger, *Poetry, Language, Thought*, trans. A. Hofstadter, New York: Harper & Row, 1975, 190-191. See also by the same author, *On the Way to Language*, trans. P. Hertz and J, Stambaugh, New York: Harper & Row, 1971.

8   M. Edwards, *Towards a Christian Poetics*, London: Macmillian, 1984, 217.

9   K. Vanhoozer, *Is There A Meaning in This Text? The Bible, the Reader, and the Morality of Literary Knowledge*, Grand Rapids: Zondervan, 1998, 205.

10   P. Ricoeur, 'The Language of Faith,' in: C. E. Reagan and D. Stewart, eds. *The Philosophy of Paul Ricoeur: An Anthology of his work*, Boston: Beacon, 1978, 230-231, seems to accept this point of view.

11   See Stiver, *Philosophy* and A. C. Thiselton, *New Horizons in Hermeneutics*, Grand Rapids: Zondervan, 1992, for erudite discussions of this topic.

In this chapter I shall not undertake the task of dealing with the breadth and diversity of all the language debates and problematics. I should like rather to address two basic, yet complicated questions related to language theory and Scripture. First, the division between religious language and other language and second, in the light of this, whether Scripture should be read as any other book or in a special manner.

1) Religious Language versus Other Types of Language

Should we consider ordinary language and religious language rivals? Does scientific language communicate more effectively? Is God language mysticism? Anthony Thiselton points out:

whereas the heart of the problem of religious language has traditionally been perceived to lie in its distinctively 'religious' character, especially since around 1967 the deepest problems of religious language are perceived to lie in the opaqueness and deceptiveness which supposedly characterize all language.[12]

In the context of this discussion, religious language is considered by some to be non-sense.[13] A requisition of special pleading is often thought to be necessary if it is going to have a legitimate place in the world and language.[14] In response to this radical

---

12   Thiselton, 'language-religious' in: A. McGrath, ed. *Blackwell Encyclopedia of Modern Christian Thought*, Oxford: Blackwell, 1993, 315-319.

13   Cuppit, 'post-Christianity,' 218-232. See Thiselton, *Interpreting God and the Postmodern Self*, Edinburgh: T&T Clark, 1995, 81-118, for an insightful analysis and critique of Cuppit's work.

14   See P. Clayton, *The Problem of God in Modern Thought*, Grand Rapids: Eerdmans, 2000, who argues that some who

separation and a privileging of ordinary or scientific language, religious language advocates may aim to enlarge the horizons of language so that religious language can be included as cognitive, or at least in some sense meaningful, without however dealing with the 'all' language problematic. The inordinate disjunction between two types of language seems to have been left intact in this scenario and it is this that I would like to explore further.[15]

Since the time of what has been referred to as positivism and perhaps even long before,[16] religious language has often been viewed as completely separate from other categories of language. The early work of L. Wittgenstein,[17] followed by A. J. Ayer[18] and others, privileged a verificationist view. Language needed to be defined according to strict empirical requirements. As Ayer is a

. . . .

doubt (following Kant) theistic language, also see difficulties with "metaphysical explanations" and a "historicity of knowledge."

15   While I agree with Thiselton that the supposed problematic today is with "all" language (see note 11 above), I would nevertheless argue that an acceptance of an absolute division between religious language and other language will not help in addressing the tyranny of this view.

16   C. E. Braaten, 'Naming the Name,' in: Braaten, ed. *Our Naming of God*, Minneapolis: Fortress, 1989, 14, argues, "the problem of language seems to be as old as creation."

17   L. Wittgenstein, *Tractatus Logico-Philosophicus*, trans. D. F. Pears and B. F. McGuinness, London: Routledge, 1961. The later Wittgenstein, in my opinion, is still empiricist in his orientation to language use or games, however he is not as reductionist as in his early work.

18   A. J. Ayer, *Language, Truth, and Logic*, New York: Dover, 1952. See D. J. O'Connor, 'Alfred Jules Ayer,' *The Encyclopedia of Philosophy 1*, New York: Macmillian, 1967, 229-231, who argues that this is "one of the most influential philosophical books of the century." See also, Thiselton, 'language-religious,' 316, "In his *Language, Truth, and Logic* of 1936, A. J. Ayer expounded what amounted to a positivist world view, but clothed in the dress of a theory of language."

major protagonist of this notion, especially concerning religious language, his position is worth citing at length:

To test whether a sentence expresses a genuine empirical hypothesis, I adopt what may be called a modified verification principle. For I require of an empirical hypothesis, not indeed that it should be conclusively verifiable, but that some possible sense-experience should be relevant to the determination of its truth or falsehood. If a putative proposition fails to satisfy this principle, and is not a tautology, then I hold that it is metaphysical, it is neither true nor false but literally senseless.

For since the religious utterances of the theist are not genuine propositions at all, they cannot stand in any logical relation to the propositions of science.

And if 'god' is a metaphysical term, then it cannot be even probable that a god exists. For to say 'God exists' is to make a metaphysical utterance which cannot be either true or false.

.... to say that something transcends the human understanding is to say that it is unintelligible. And what is unintelligible cannot significantly be described. But if one allows that it is impossible to define God in intelligible terms, then one is allowing that it is impossible for a sentence both to be significant and to be about God.[19]

Ayer's concoction of an effacing of metaphysics and an embrace of scientific—positivistic analysis attempts to render religious

19   Ayer, *Language*, 31, 115, 117-118.

language non-sense. This point of view has undoubtedly contributed to the trend of a denial of metaphysics in any form,[20] as well as to a general suspicion towards the referential capacity of all language in the wake of its failure, yet the contemporary version of this rejection and skepticism is more entangled in theories of language than in scientific—empirical presuppositions per se.

It has become indispensable in the light of this emphasis on language theory and its relation to God, Scripture, metaphysics, and intelligibility, among other issues, that those who practice biblical hermeneutics be aware of how theories of language are intertwined with and have an influence on the task of biblical interpretation. Language theory is connected to a view of the world and reality that is often the underlying force behind such a theory.[21] As this is the case, it is essential that Christian interpreters of Scripture be encouraged to re-think language theories, including their own, in the recognition that such theories have a premise which is connected to a world-

---

20   J. M. Soskice, *Metaphor and Religious Language*, Oxford: Oxford University Press, 1995, 144.

21   M. Devitt and K. Sterelny, *Language and Reality: An Introduction to the Philosophy of Language*, Oxford: Blackwell, 1999, Second ed. 236-237, comment in regard to Ayer and the positivists, "So, at the same time the positivists are rejecting the metaphysical dispute about the nature of reality, they are making a strong metaphysical assumption about reality: it consists only of the given. Despite their disavowals, they are committed to a powerful and, we claim, thoroughly false metaphysics." While agreeing with this evaluation and critique, I would nevertheless disagree with these two scholars on their approach to the problem of language, which is entirely "naturalistic" in both the epistemological and metaphysical sense. See also, *Language*, 9-10.

view.[22] How does a view of the world 'count' when it comes to a language-view? World-view analysis will not inevitably decide if a language theory is God affirming or denying, yet world-view considerations will give some useful indications as to the merit, or lack of thereof, of a language theory for the Christian art and action of interpreting God, the world, and the self. Responsible Christian scholarship will endeavor to detect which world-views are attached to which theories and whether or not these are hermeneutically in accord with Scripture.

There is no question today of whether Ayer's language theory, or his world-view for that matter, were justifiable. They have been rightly critiqued and one would suppose bypassed on the grounds that the verification principle itself is non-empirical.[23] However, what interests me at this stage is not the validity of the critique, but the powerful residue of the theory that seems to remain in spite of it.[24] One still finds, for example, as influen-

---

22   A. Wolters, *Creation Regained*, Carlisle: Paternoster, 1996, 1-11 on the importance of Christians thinking world-view. See also, Devitt and Sterelny, *Language*, 237, who point out that, "one cannot theorize about anything, least of all language, without implicit commitment to a view of the world." Also, Ricoeur, *History and Truth*, trans. C. Kelbley, Evanston: Northwestern University Press, 1965, 193, states: "Every philosophical attitude flows from a *Weltanschuung*, from a certain vision of the 'world.'" *(Italics his)*.

23   O'Connor, 'Alfred Jules Ayer,' *The Encyclopedia of Philosophy 1*, 230, asserts that Ayer's view has "been shown to be faulty in admitting as meaningful metaphysical statements of precisely the kind that the principle is designed to outlaw." Also, Stiver, *Philosophy*, 44-46, points out that one significant factor in the theory's diminishing influence was the internal critique from the positivists themselves.

24   J. H. Gill, *On Knowing God: New Directions for the Future of Theology*, Philadelphia: Westminster, 1981, 36. See also, Thiselton, *New Horizons*, 20, who provocatively suggests an analogy between

tial a scholar as Paul Ricoeur generally accepting that there is an unmitigated difference between religious language and other language,[25] although he forcefully joins the critique of the positivist position in other respects.[26] In my opinion, Ricoeur attempts to make religious language credible within what he sees as a 'process of secularization,' a world of technical, factual, and scientific language. In some sense, I share his evaluation and a concern over the loss of the sacred, yet differ in the way to address the problem. His argument is that religious language has a right or even a priority over other language and therefore has at least a legitimate place along side it. This view however, assumes that other language types are unable to speak God and this leaves Ricoeur reducing God language to the poetic-symbolic.[27] On the issue of religious language, it is argued that Ricoeur's orientation is more anthropological (human possibilities), than theological (about God).[28]

. . . .

Ayer and his world-view, "positivism in linguistic dress" and Barthes, Derrida, among others, who propose "a post-modernist world-view in semiotic dress."

25   Ricoeur, 'The Language of Faith,' 223-238. Also, *History and Truth*, 165-191.

26   Ricoeur, 'Toward A Hermeneutic of the Idea of Revelation,' in: L. S. Mudge, ed. *Essays on Biblical Interpretation*, 100-104. See the comments by J. Fodor, *Christian Hermeneutics*, Oxford: Oxford University Press, 1995, 147-171, who perceives something of a "residual positivism" in Ricoeur's view of language, while he nevertheless points out some of his differences with a positivistic outlook.

27   Ricoeur, 'Toward A Hermeneutic,' 100-104, and 'Biblical Hermeneutics,' *Semeia* 4, (1975), 29-148. This does not mean, in Ricoeur's orientation, that poetic language is non-cognitive or non-referential.

28   See Vanhoozer, *Biblical Narrative in the Philosophy of Paul Ricoeur: A Study in hermeneutics and theology*, Cambridge:

A variety of responses to Ayer and those who adopted similar views of language have developed, but I shall briefly focus on only two of them. In her influential book *Metaphor and Religious Language*,[29] Janet Martin Soskice points out two such ripostes that influenced biblical interpretation: Christian empiricism and idealism.

According to Soskice, Christian empiricism was proposed by Ian T. Ramsey[30] who attempted to show that religious language was cognitively credible on the basis of empirical arguments, which would in turn in his opinion, lead to the re-animation of metaphysics. Ramsey recognized that if this was to happen there needed to be an adequate explanation of reference in religious language. One of the ways he formulated this was in terms of 'cosmic disclosure' affirming that this type of confrontation might function in a positive manner for objective reference and claims of transcendence. One of Ramsey's difficulties in this project was being too empirical, or at least being inconsistent with his empirical orientations. Soskice states:

His difficulty is this - he relies on his empiricism to ground his reference, but he is not justified in terms of the same empiricism in

....

Cambridge University Press, 1990, 120-122; 236-238. For another view, see G. J. Laughery, *Living Hermeneutics: An Analysis and Evaluation of Paul Ricoeur's Contribution to Biblical Hermeneutics*, Lanham: University Press of America, 2002, 115-120.

29   Soskice, *Metaphor*, has done much to dispel the illusions that scientific and theological models and metaphors are completely incongruent. Her insights, in this context, make a valuable contribution to a theory of language. I am in her debt for these thoughts on Christian empiricism and the notions of idealism.

30   I. T. Ramsey, *Religious Language: An Empirical Placing of Theological Phrases; Christian Empiricism*, London: SCM, 1974.

developing the 'disclosure event' with models of God as husband, king, landlord, shepherd, or judge. The disclosure is simply a point of reference with no content and, to be consistent with his empiricism .... Ramsey should restrict his claims to what is observable, but this he plainly does not wish to do.[31]

If there is no reason why Christians should eschew empirical reference claims, it is crucial however that they recognize any exclusive focus on them leads to reductionism, which in turn diminishes the broader based assertions of Scripture that God communicates in a diversity of ways. An over-emphasis on solely empirical concerns results in biblical interpretation being forced into a frame that is unable to contain the picture. Ramsey sought to establish the cognitive character of religious language in the midst of the era of positivism and falsification, rather than questioning the validity of the world-view presuppositions underlying the claims that there was a valid exclusivity between religious language and other types of language in the first place.

Soskice argues that with the failure of empiricist theology, and in the face of skepticism towards cognitive models or claims for religious language, one may find something of an explanation for an idealist thesis.[32] In her opinion, this relates to a broad point of view which can characterize religious language as personal, affective, or evocational. Religious language, it is thought, has an impact in an existential sense as it addresses

---

31   Soskice, *Metaphor*, 146.
32   Ibid., 147. While it is true that Soskice is discussing scientific models she herself makes an application to the theist and the Christian in this regard.

the human situation, but it does not 'depict reality.'[33] Such language has some form of anthropological merit, but it is theologically empty. In this context, the transcendent—immanent God of Scripture disappears behind a cacophony of fictive or human constructs which are continuously recycled as they fail to have any capacity to refer outside themselves. God is so far away that language can never begin to speak God. Biblical interpretation risks becoming a shadow desperately in search of a form that lacks any stability.

The problematic, as I see it, is that both of these developments accept the fundamental division between religious language and other types of language. Christian empiricism seeks to respond to positivistic empiricism with empiricism on its own terms, attempting to observably show that religious language is just as meaningful and cognitive as other language. Idealism argues that there is no need to respond to empirical claims and criteria as religious language should not have to measure up to such demands. In being freed from these requirements religious language may speak in an entirely different way, hence there is no need to seek to justify it as cognitive or even referentially meaning-full.

In the light of the weaknesses in these two responses to Ayer and his view of language, which in some sense remain relevant in our own context, Soskice appeals to and calls for a theological realism. While not agreeing with all her arguments and conclusions,[34] she has done much to advance the language

---

33   Ibid., 97-117.
34   Ibid., 147-161. I do agree with Soskice that a theological realism should neither be dogmatic nor presumptuous and that a realist perspective accommodates figurative speech which is

discussion. I shall sketch out below a somewhat different angle on theological realism and its application to language.

Does the embracing of an *exclusive* division between different types of language force biblical scholarship into choosing between the false options of religious language versus other categories of language?[35] In my opinion, a theological perspective contributes to a unifying of language that does not discount its diversity. On this account, theology legitimately addresses the issue of the 'all' language problematic.[36] This can be framed in an 'either-or' manner. Scripture makes a powerful and pivotal proposal: God is there as opposed to not being there. If God is there, this then opens the possibility of a 'both-and' paradigm for the world and language that may be described in the following way.

Scripture, for example, affirms that God exists *both* outside the world and language use (transcendent),[37] *and* also that God comes into the world[38] and language use through speaking in

---

reality depicting. I also agree that a realist position holds that the world informs our theory, however I am not convinced that our theories may never adequately describe the world. My view would be that it is possible to sufficiently describe the world and that most of the time that is practically what happens. In those cases description is adequate.

35   While no one denies some distinction, as with French and English, is there not also a primordial relationship that has been underplayed with regard to its place in the world and language? Religious language is distinct from other language, yet it is also related to it.

36   See the quote from Thiselton above.

37   F. Watson, *Text, Church, and World. Biblical Interpretation in Theological Perspective*, Edinburgh: T&T Clark, 1994, 144.

38   Braaten, 'Naming the Name,' 29, argues the problem of contemporary thinking about God is expressed in a "great divide." There are those who see anthropomorphic language about God as beyond all concreteness "rapt in mystical silence" and those

creation, to people, and through Christ (immanent).[39] There is no warrant to collapse these two truths into one, nor is it necessary to wholly distinguish them, as in one fashion or another empiricism and idealist notions tend to do. A definite tension embedded on the level of God and the world, language, and human beings, points toward the possibility of a relation-distinction between the identity of God and language. Tension in this Scriptural sense is to be embraced, not rejected. To say it another way, God is outside — *beyond* language, but can be said inside — *within* language. This is precisely because God in Scripture is revealed in language, although never confused with it. The point here is that God is not reduced to language, but is *both* related to *and* distinct from it as God, hence the relation-distinction tension. Furthermore, I would argue this holds true for the world and for human beings. God is *both* related to the world as creation, *and* also distinct from it as God and, God is *both* related to human beings, *and* also distinct from them as God.[40]

....

who follow "the incarnational current deep into history, into the concreteness of human flesh" - God incarnate in Jesus. Braaten rightly affirms the latter, but in my opinion too exclusively, thereby lacking an emphasis on a creational and eschatological perspective.

39   E. Jüngel, *God as the Mystery of the World*, trans. D. L. Guder, Edinburgh: T&T Clark, 1983, 288, remarks with regard to Christ, "The translation of the model of human speech to God is based on the certainty that God has shown himself to be human in the execution of his divinity. To think of him as one who speaks, to speak of him as one who speaks, is not a 'dogmatic anthropomorphism,' which comes too close to God, but rather the result of that *event* in which God becomes accessible as God in language, which the Bible calls *revelation*."

40   See C. Gunton, *The One, the Three and the Many: God, Creation and the Culture of Modernity*, Cambridge: Cambridge University

A Scriptured portrayal of this tension relates to daily life, the land, work, justice, economics, social contexts, etc. The Scripture writes to the whole of life not some sequestered area designated 'religious.'[41] Whether scientific, ordinary, or religious, 'all' language has a capacity, in a meaningful, referential, dynamic manner, to point back to the Creator who made the world and human beings as images of God. Particles, quarks, atoms, and rock, fortress, shelter may all recount something of the complexity and character of God the Creator.[42] Why should any of these, in their specific contexts, be prohibited from referring to God in a general context? What is one to make of the most sophisticated geometrical language formulations? Why should they be forbidden from having the Creator as their referent? Such language types, while often used in specific scientific or mathematical contexts, may also refer to God in a more general creational perspective. As the world is not merely one's own but God's, language boundaries can be refigured. Scientific and religious languages are not so absolutely divided as Christians may often

. . . .

Press, 1993, 167, 207-219, on the relation-distinction between God, world, and being.

41   C. Wright, *Living as the People of God*, Leicester: IVP, 1983. See also, Wolters, *Creation*, 7, who rightly argues, "Scripture speaks centrally to everything in our life and world, including technology, and economics and science."

42   Ricoeur, *History and Truth*, 193, argues, "in the eyes of the psalmist: it is the trees which "clap their hands" and not the electrons and neutrons." While this is true, perhaps it is not necessary to paint the picture so reductionistically. If one considers the creational perspective that God made the world and everything in it, as affirmed, for example, in Paul's discussion with the Athenians (recounted in Luke's narrative: Acts 17: 22-34), there is no necessity to exclude the language and reality of electrons and neutrons from pointing to the creator God.

have been led to suppose.[43] They are *both* related and *distinct* on a creational level. What I want to stress here, from a Scriptural perspective, is that language is creational in that it enters the world through the world's createdness. As the world is given by God, so is language. Human language in the world then, refers back to its Creator and is first of all an attribute of the speaking God who is revealed as the Great Speaker.[44]

On a creational register language is language, as for example, experience is experience. While it is true there are distinct types, this does not signify that one type is utterly disjointed from the other on the level of language or experience. All language has cognitive and non-cognitive, literal, metaphorical, analogical, private and public spheres which are related to and dependent on the contexts in which language is used.

The perspective of the relatedness of all language then, on the level of creation, does not necessitate an obliterating of distinctions. Language games or understanding the world as linguistic may, in some sense, be viewed positively from a Christian standpoint.[45] There is no question that there are

---

43   Stiver, *Philosophy*, 196, states, "Perhaps the most remarkable implication of recent developments for religious language is the affirmation that despite irreducible imprecision and metaphorical language, religious language is communicable and understandable. Even if religious language possesses more indeterminate and figurative language it is not so unlike other language, even scientific language."

44   Vanhoozer, *Is There A Meaning?*, 205. See also, Milbank, *The Word Made Strange, Theology, Language, Culture*, Oxford: Blackwell, 1997, 29, who argues that human language utterance reflects the divine creative act.

45   Thiselton, 'Language and Meaning in Religion,' in: C. Brown, ed. *NIDNTT, Vol. 3*, Exeter: Paternoster, 1978 & 1986, 1123-1146.

different types of language use and that these are relevant in their own specific contexts.[46] Distinctions may be perceived as a good thing and a beautiful dimension of creativity. What often happens however, is that these contexts are thought to become the totality of language, thereby negating any horizons larger than their own network or language game. If this is the case, language becomes the sole vehicle for understanding, explanation, and new understanding, rather than one important, but not comprehensive reality—world identifier.[47] If there is no referent outside of one's language games, networks, and the linguisticality of the world the hermeneutical circle is indeed vicious and not productive.[48]

---

46   Ibid., 1123-1146, esp. 1132, where Thiselton argues that religious language 'is not necessarily a special kind of language, but is ordinary language put to a special kind of use.'

47   Laughery, *Living Hermeneutics*, 55-91.

48   Ricoeur, *The Conflict of Interpretations*, D. Ihde, ed. Evanston: Northwestern University Press, 1969, 298, argues, "This circle is not vicious; still less is it deadly." and 389, "The hermeneutic circle can be stated roughly as follows. To understand, it is necessary to believe; to believe, it is necessary to understand. This formulation is still too psychological. For behind believing there is the primacy of faith over faith; and behind understanding there is the primacy of exegesis and its method over the naïve reading of the text. This means that the genuine hermeneutical circle is not psychological but methodological. It is the circle constituted by the object that regulates faith and the method that regulates understanding. There is a circle because the exegete is not his own master. What he wants to understand is what the text says; the task of understanding is therefore governed by what is at issue in the text itself. Christian hermeneutics is moved by the announcement which is at issue in the text." According to Ricoeur, 'Toward A Hermeneutic,' 103, "The proposed world that in biblical language is called a new creation, a new Covenant, the Kingdom of God, is the 'issue' of the biblical text unfolded in front of this text."

A major difficulty concerning the problematic of 'all' language, in my opinion, resides in this previously described claustrophobia. That is, there is supposedly no way out of distinction. One is caught within a web of distinct language uses that never relate or cohere. Each language game has only its own specific rules which are not subject to any general ones. In this plot distinction reigns, and relation is underplayed or even thought to be non-existent. Yet for all the supposed flexibility here the result is disconcertingly one dimensional.

The problem is not with distinct language categories per se, but with not re-connecting the distinctions to relatedness and viewing both as emanating from God the Creator.[49] The fascinating intricacy of both *relation* and *distinction*, in finding its raison d'être in the being, character, and complexity of God, must be allowed to play itself out in a positive 'both-and' tension, which better explains the world and the phenomena of language than reductionistic polarizations. The creator God, who is capable of creating the universe in all its complexity, explodes such reductionism in having spoken open the world for investigation, creativity, participation, and discovery, which in turn produces language use of both a *related* and a *distinct* manner.

This framing of God's transcendence and immanence, in spoken penetration of the created world,[50] opens up possibilities

---

49   I would propose that the Babel event in Gen. 11, often understood as the root of language distinction, might be better explained as the root of language confusion. Gen. 10 seems to affirm that distinction was already there pre-Babel.

50   See Milbank, *The Word*, 74-78, for an illuminating discussion of Hamann's views of language, creation, and God's transcendence. In addition, Watson, *Text, Church*, 137-153, on language, God, and creation.

for an 'all' language perspective through a creational context. This is embedded in the Creator-creature relation-distinction (Gen. 1-2). Furthermore, God's transcendence and immanence spokenly revealed in the saving Word (Jn. 1) and the event of Pentecost (Acts 2) opens 'new' possibilities for language in a salvific context (Eph. 5.1-20). Perhaps, the great contemporary language debate centers on the answer to the ancient query, 'Did God really say?' (Gen. 3.1). As suspicion reigns over trust, human beings are devastatingly broken, language misfires, communication and relationship are shrouded in obscurity, and left a mere shadow of what they were.[51] God's goal through Christ in vanquishing the latter however, is not focused on a re-deeming of language, but on the hope of a transformation of the whole world (Rev. 21.1-27), including people, and through people, language, communication, and relationship.[52] This per-spective situates language in a creational, salvific, and escha-tological context which recognizes its value and importance, without granting it a power or status it does not deserve. Lan-guage is continually at the frontiers of language[53] and is being

51   There is always the possibility that people speaking language misfire. Should this surprise us? Meanings and referents are partially opaque, yet context can help in diminishing this to the sufficient degree that language often functions accurately, but never perfectly. See D. A. Carson, *The Gagging of God*, Leicester: IVP, 1996, 102-105, on valid communication.

52   In this case, language has no ontological status of its own. The Word in John's gospel, for example, seeks to redeem people as a person/God, not language. Language, in a Scriptural context, is always related to a person/being, never an entity in and of itself or the totality of any person/being.

53   Ricoeur, *Interpretation Theory: Discourse and the Surplus of Meaning*, Fort Worth: Texas Christian Uinversity Press, 1976, 20, states, "Language is not a world of its own. It is not even a world."

framed as a traitor when scholars argue that it refers only to itself.[54]

A crucial task for Christian scholarship, as it aims to faithfully interpret the biblical text, is to make effective and rigorous theological contributions to redrawing the boundaries of language theory. I am not intending to say that Scripture presents a detailed philosophy of language, but perhaps biblical scholars have underplayed the possibility that it may provide a paradigmatic world-view perspective that gives an orientation to the world, language, and the whole of life. Al Wolters puts it this way:

[b]iblical faith in fact involves a worldview, at least implicitly and in principle. The central notion of creation (a given order of reality), fall (human mutiny at the root of all perversion of the given order) and redemption (unearned restoration of the order in Christ) are cosmic and transformational in their implications. Together with other basic elements … these central ideas … give believers the fundamental outline of a completely anti-pagan Weltanschauung, a worldview which provides the interpretive framework for history, society, culture, politics, and everything else that enters human experience.[55]

. . . .

Ricoeur's point here is that language is always dependent on something else. Also see, *Interpretation Theory*, 15-16, where he argues for the miracle of communicative meaning becoming public.

54   Crossan, *The Dark Interval. Towards A Theology of Story*, Niles: Argus, 1975, 40-41.

55   A. Wolters, 'Gustavo Gutiérrez,' in: J. Klapwijk, S. Griffioen, and G. Groenewoud, eds. *Bringing into Captivity Every Thought*, Lanham: university Press of America, 1991, 237.

It is vitally important to evaluate philosophical, literary, hermeneutical, and language world-views in the light of the biblical text and in so doing to be better able to elucidate their advantages and disadvantages for the faithful art and action of biblical interpretation.[56] While it is true, following Wittgenstein, that 'what we cannot speak about we must pass over in silence',[57] one might complement this with, 'and where we can sufficiently speak we must.'

2) Should Scripture be Read as any other Book or in a special manner?

There has been a fair amount of lively debate over this question.[58] My aim is to address this controversy, in its contemporary context, through an elucidation of what Ricoeur and others have referred to as the question of general and regional hermeneutics, or another way of stating it, philosophical and biblical hermeneutics.[59] I shall primarily focus on the work of

---

56   See Laughery, *Living Hermeneutics*, 105-106. Perhaps, as an unfortunate result of over-specialization, biblical scholars often pay little attention to the ways in which philosophical-general hermeneutics in-forms or de-forms a reading of the biblical text, while philosophers rarely engage themselves with biblical-regional hermeneutics, thereby inadvertently, (or perhaps otherwise) risking the loss of a more in-formed or less de-formed reading of that very philosophy.

57   Wittgenstein, *Tractatus*, 74.

58   Laughery, *Living Hermeneutics*, 92-106, for a fuller account than can be undertaken here.

59   Ricoeur, 'Philosophical Hermeneutics and Biblical Hermeneutics,' in: *From Text to Action*, trans. K. Blamey and J. B. Thompson, Evanston: Northwestern University Press, 1991, 89-101. See also, H. Frei, 'The "Literal Reading" of Biblical Narrative in the Christian Tradition,' in: F. McConnell, ed. *The Bible and*

Ricoeur, as in my opinion, it can make a useful contribution to this question. The dispute concerning whether one reads Scripture as any other book or in a special way is intricately linked to the hermeneutical orientations just mentioned and to the discussion of language addressed in the first part of this chapter. Language, reading Scripture, and philosophical — biblical hermeneutics are not entirely unrelated worlds of investigation. While respecting their differences and in no way attempting to cancel them out, their relationship also needs to be recognized. Polarized viewpoints, without warrant, or a sophisticated synthesis, for its own sake, are in danger of short circuiting the hermeneutical enterprise. Does a creational perspective play a role in this debate? How might a 'both-and' trajectory work its way out with respect to reading the Bible and what are the implications for biblical hermeneutics?

Some have argued that of the two hermeneutical orientations a Christian perspective should privilege a biblical—theological, rather than a philosophical hermeneutics,[60] or even that the way the Bible is read should be the way that all other texts are read.[61] It is often maintained that Ricoeur gives precedence to a

. . . .

the Narrative Tradition, Oxford: Oxford University Press, 1986, 36-77; G. Lindbeck, The Nature of Doctrine: Religion and Theology in a Postliberal Age, Philadelphia: Westminster, 1984, and D. H. Kelsey, The Uses of Scripture in Recent Theology, Philadelphia: Fortress, 1975.

60   Watson, Text, Church, 1-2.

61   Vanhoozer, Is There A Meaning in This Text?, 379, "Christian doctrine, I have claimed, has hermeneutical significance. I prefer to say, not that we should read the Bible like any other book, but that we should read every other book as we have learned to read the Bible, namely, in a spirit of understanding that lets the text be what it is and do what it intends."

philosophical over a biblical hermeneutics.[62] Allegedly, Ricoeur supports his biblical hermeneutics with a philosophical point of view that jeopardizes the true referent of the biblical story.[63] That is, Ricoeur has attempted to re-frame the ancient text in more contemporary categories in order to make it compatible with current philosophical concerns and queries.

I would suggest the debate over biblical and philosophical hermeneutics might move toward greater clarity if one remembers to differentiate between a reader's imposition of a general—philosophical hermeneutics and having one in the first place (which may or may not then be modified as a result of reading Scripture). Will an interpreter simply impose the general—philosophical hermeneutic and snuff out the flaming arrow of the sense and referent of the biblical text—God, world, Christ, self and other, etc. - or will this arrow enlighten enough to explain that this is God's Spirit illuminated word, world, creation, not one's own, and thereby transfigure a reader's general—philosophical hermeneutics into a biblical hermeneutics, demonstrating that one is obliged to come under an authority greater than oneself?

There is no doubt a complex inter-relationship between philosophical and biblical hermeneutics in the thought of Ricoeur.[64] Does this presume, as Frei and others argue, that he

---

62   Frei, 'Literal Reading', esp. 45, 50, 56 for a critique of Ricoeur on this. Also Vanhoozer, *Biblical Narrative*, 148-150.

63   Frei, 'Literal Reading,' 50. See also, W. C. Placher, 'Paul Ricoeur and Postliberal Theology: A Conflict of Interpretations,' *Modern Theology* 4, (1988) 35-52.

64   See M. I. Wallace, *The Second Naiveté, Barth, Ricoeur and the New Yale Theology*, Macon: Mercer University Press, 1990,

gives more weight to the philosophical?[65] Ricoeur affirms that the philosophical pole begins the movement to the biblical. In his opinion, the same categories of a 'work, writing, world of text, distanciation and appropriation' apply to both poles.[66] However, Ricoeur's position is that in dialogue with the unique character of the biblical text the movement inverses, eventually resulting in the subordination of the philosophical to the biblical. The biblical overpowers the philosophical.[67]

In my view, this is because the explanation of God, the world (God's creation), the human condition (a broken God image), history (God's mighty acts), salvation (Christ), the future (new heavens and earth) are utterly and magnificently unique. The biblical text has the capacity, because of these truths among others, to lead one from understanding, through explanation, to new understanding which culminates in a knowledge of the truth and a saving relationship with God.

On the one hand, Ricoeur's view affirms a hermeneutical motion from the philosophical to the biblical, while on the other, philosophical hermeneutics gradually functions within the sphere of a text related biblical hermeneutics. I shall briefly focus on three points of this gradual movement in Ricoeur's hermeneutics: a 'confession of faith,' asseverated in the forms of biblical discourse, 'the world of the text' and the 'naming of God.'[68]

. . . .

27-103. Also, Laughery, *Living Hermeneutics*, 91-121 and 172-195. Vanhoozer, *Biblical Narrative*, 119-272.

65   Fodor, *Christian Hermeneutics*, 258-330, has an excellent discussion of Frei and Ricoeur.

66   Ricoeur, 'Philosophical and Biblical,' 89-90.

67   Ibid., 89-90. See also, Ricoeur, 'Toward A Hermeneutic,' 104.

68   Ricoeur, 'Hermeneutique - Les finalités de l'exégèse biblique,' in: *La Bible en philosophie*, Paris: Cerf, 1993, 27-51, formulates his

Firstly, Ricoeur views the confession of faith, in the biblical text, as interwoven with its forms of discourse.[69] As a result of this vision, it can be said that the biblical text has a structure, genres, such as narrative, parable, gospel, prophetic, etc., while at the same moment however, it is also a declaration of faith.[70] For Ricoeur, it is precisely this declaration that challenges philosophical hermeneutics, resulting in its eventual surpassing, but not effacing by biblical hermeneutics.

In Ricoeur's argumentation the inversing, and eventual subordinating of philosophical hermeneutics to biblical hermeneutics, comes about through the message or content of the biblical text as expressed in its diversity of forms of discourse. Form and content, in this sense, can be said to synchronize, yet this synchronization does not produce an annihilation of either one or the other. Such is the case because Scripture's content can be identified by the form (narrative, etc.), but the content (God the great actor of deliverance) is not merely the form.

Secondly, 'the world of the text,' as the world of the bibli-

. . . .

views on "la lecture savante and la lecture confessante" and gives an insightful articulation of biblical genres and the theological import of their confessing characteristics.

69   See chapter 5 below, Engaging the Parables of Jesus, for how this pertains to the parables.

70   Ricoeur, 'Philosophy and Religious Language,' *Journal of Religion* 54 (1974), 71-85, esp. 84-85 where faith is related to a logic of superabundance. "... the thematic of faith escapes from hermeneutics and testifies to the fact that the former is neither the first nor last word." There is a need for a reliance on a "constantly renewed interpretation of the sign-events reported by the writings, such as the Exodus in the Old Testament and the Resurrection in the New Testament."

cal text. Ricoeur calls this 'thing' of the text,[71] the 'object' of hermeneutics.[72] Hermeneutics, in the first instance, is to be an explaining of the text and the world of the text as a proposed world of possibility and possible habitation. Many texts, it can be said, present a world, but the specificity of biblical discourse, as Ricoeur affirms, is to be found in the emblematic characteristic of its referent 'God' and in the presentation of a new world, new birth, new covenant.[73]

Thirdly, there is a biblical text resistance situated in the fact that in the naming of God, the word 'God', cannot be reduced to a philosophical concept of 'being' as it always says more than this. Ricoeur appeals to the word as presupposing a total context under which, and towards which, all the diversity of biblical discourses gravitate. To understand this word involves a supervening of the arrow of sense orchestrated by God. For Ricoeur, this 'arrow of sense' asseverates a twofold force: firstly, a re-assembling of the entire signification generated by the biblical discourses, incomplete though they may be, and secondly, the aperture of a vista that eludes the closure of discourse.[74] The naming of God, in Scripture, relates to God's initiative and objectifying of sense.

---

71   See N. Wolterstorff, *Divine Discourse, Philosophical Reflections on the Claim that God Speaks*, Cambridge: Cambridge University Press, 1995, 130-152, for a critique of Ricoeur's emphasis on the meaning of the text at the expense of the author's intention. Vanhoozer, *Is There A Meaning?* 106-111, addresses this question with much erudition. See also Laughery, *Living Hermeneutics*, 292-321 and chapter 4 below, Authors, Readers, and Texts.

72   Ricoeur, 'Philosophical and Biblical,' 95.

73   Ibid., 97. In addition, Ricoeur, 'Philosophy and Religious Language,' 71-85.

74   Ricoeur, 'Philosophical and Biblical,' 97-98.

According to Ricoeur, on the grounds of these three points among others, regional—biblical hermeneutics becomes the organon for general—philosophical hermeneutics. It seems however, in my opinion, that this can only be confirmed through the Spirit illuminated Scripture and its reader in reading the author's literary act inscribed in the biblical text. This scenario works out in the following way. Every interpreter comes to the Bible with a general—philosophical point of view when they begin to read it. One's reading the biblical text does not make this be the case, as it is already in place on a creational level before one ever reads Scripture.[75] Yet this reading does count for the reader, not in the sense that one makes the biblical text what it is when read, no more than one makes a car what it is when looking both ways before crossing the street. The reader is always both *related* to what is read and *distinct* from it, just as the person crossing the street is related to the car, and distinct from it. The point here is that these relations-distinctions can be said to be true for human beings at the practical level on general hermeneutical grounds. I would argue this is because it is God's world (although it may not always be recognized for what it is), even before one reads the Bible to discover that this is the case. It is nevertheless, the biblical text that explains how and why the world is the way it is. In moving from general to regional hermeneutical grounds there is then an overcoming and re-framing of the general as Scripture explains that

---

75   Interpretation is rooted in the situatedness of the interpreter, however it is not actualized only by this, but also by the created world which precedes it. Interpretation takes place within the borders of creational limits. No interpreter, at least that I know of, begins the hermeneutical journey grounded in the biblical text.

this is God's creation. Biblical scholars too often underplay a biblical world-view perspective that frames a place for the scientific, language orientated, and philosophical approaches to the world as it is God's created world. These valid enterprises however, need to be put into dialogue with Spirit illuminated Scripture if they are to have a possibility of both affirming and critiquing their various positions on criteria both related to and distinct from themselves. This is essential if they are to move from understanding, through explanation, to new understanding that it is ultimately God who gives science, philosophy, and language their raison d'être in the first place. As Acts 17:22-34, in a fascinating coup de force affirms, God has created the world and everything in it and it is in God that humans live and move and are.

I would argue Scripture may *both* be read as any other text, *and* not be read as any other text. Either a one dimensional forcing, a synthesis that exclusively fuses these two together, or an antithesis that keeps them entirely apart seems inadequate on the level of the complexity of creation. There is interconnection without effacement. The intriguing value of a 'both-and' approach to this question, as has already been argued with reference to language, is that it respects a creational relation-distinction, symmetry—asymmetry dynamic on the register of God, Scripture, the world, and language, which culminates in a tension that neither de-prioritizes the biblical, nor dissolves the philosophical.

All texts are texts and their authors may indicate, in one way or another, that this is God's world, but not all authored texts claim to be revelation illuminated by the Spirit.[76] Even though the former is the case, the Bible remains a special text, not just one of many texts. Authored Scripture's Spirit illuminated recounting of events in history, its theological configuration, its referent God, its creation—salvific—eschatological focus, its canonical form, etc. all render it unique. The Scripture merits being read as a special book. It is still true, however, that the Bible is a text like other texts: genres, work, written, etc. and therefore that it should be read as any other text might be. On one level the Bible is a special book, on another level it is book like any other. This perspective acknowledges a space for both a biblical—regional and a philosophical—general hermeneutics and a tension between them that is interactive and productive.

My contention is that to force this issue into an 'either-or' where it is not warranted may result in a underplaying of the complexity of Scripture, creation, and the concurrent relation-distinction that has already been developed with respect to the problematic of language. While it is true that the Bible presents God as 'either' there 'or' not there, the Bible is not God and therefore does not 'either-or' frame the question of the Bible being read as a special book or like any other. Perhaps, as with language, a 'both-and' perspective is in order, but if this is the case it must be clear where the relations-distinctions stand.

The relevance of this for biblical hermeneutics moves along the following lines. A biblical world-view presents the hermeneutical venture as a living one in motion. Interpreters are situated in the created world, move to the authored Spirit illumi-

---

76   Gunton, *A Brief Theology of Revelation*, Edinburgh: T&T Clark, 1995, 64-82.

nated biblical text, and potentially move back to the world with a biblical view of it. In other words, there is a movement from understanding, through explanation, to new understanding. However, the trajectory does not end here in a biblical perspective. A living hermeneutics in motion only comes to its realized, yet provisionally mediated closure, when the biblical text is acted or lived out into the world. It is only in this sense that a contribution to the transformation of the world begins and can be brought to finite completion.

Biblical hermeneutics does not culminate with the linking of author and reader or the connecting of the world of text and the world of reader,[77] but with the hermeneutical Spirit illuminated "what" read and Spirit acted on, which has *transforming world power* as it continues its motion through the text to the reader, and through the reader out into the animate world. It is only when this motion reaches the world, not just the world of the reader, that a living hermeneutics motion is then re-animated back through the hermeneutical circle in a broad sense. The animate world, in its relation and distinction to both biblical text and reader, is a hermeneutical factor that demands consideration. The world of the text and the world of the reader then must finally be in dialogue with the world God has created. This hermeneutics in motion however, is envisaged as stratified, neither static, nor iniquitous. In this context,

---

77   Ricoeur and LaCocque, *Penser la Bible*, Paris: Seuil, 1998. *Thinking Biblically, Exegetical and Hermeneutical Studies*, trans. D. Pellauer, Chicago: University of Chicago Press, 1998, ix-xix, who, I believe, over-emphasize the readerly end. See also, Ricoeur, 'Life: A Story in Search of a Narrator,' in: M. J. Valdés, ed. *A Ricoeur Reader: Reflection and Imagination*, Toronto: Toronto University Press, 1991, 423-437.

hermeneutical motion is to be understood as living and having the capacity to affect the world.

While it is true that the goal of understanding and explanation is what has been done in the text, which then for a reader has the possibility of becoming new understanding (Ricoeur's passionate claim), this new understanding also calls for an engagement with God and the world in order to evaluate and cultivate its authenticity. If this is the case, the hermeneutical venture is not entirely a private matter between text and reader, but in addition to this, it relates to the world which is distinct from, yet related to both.

In this sense, the biblical text through its readers, must be acted out into the animate world, (which speaks back), if anything other than self-transformation is to be hoped for that world. Ricoeur's use of the biblical realities of new covenant, the Kingdom of God, new creation are neither merely poetic possibilities, nor are they solely concerned with self-understanding (they do pertain to and are for both) in the biblical text. Such biblical realities however, also aim at a transforming the totality of the world, not merely the one of the reader.

Conclusion

The issues of language and reading Scripture addressed in this chapter are indeed something of a minefield. In my opinion, those interested in interpreting Scripture better, cannot afford to avoid the arduous questions that language, philosophy, and hermeneutics pose for biblical interpretation. It is essential to be keenly aware that each of these will have an effect, sometimes positive, sometimes negative, on how one interprets the biblical text. A variety of language proposals, philosophical overtures, or hermeneutical directives are simply anti-God and must be identified and critiqued on their own grounds, without adopting an anti-Christian methodology.

Wolters, Ricoeur, and Thiselton have all pointed out that world-views are always connected to philosophical perspectives and language theories. Discernment, for a Christian perspective is indispensable, not only when it comes to the evaluation of language claims and philosophical statements, but also with respect to the underlying world-views that are an integral part of them.

The validity of the Christian faith will only suffer should interpreters assume that the minefield is of no concern to them.[78] There remains much work to be done in terms of engaging previous and emergent points of view in all these fields if Christians are going to have a role in developing a theory of language and better ways of reading and living Scripture out into the world.

Language theory, as explained in the Introduction, is much debated in our contemporary context. In some circles, it seems to be all that matters. Everything is language and language is often considered meaningless. It was only a short step from Ayer's overstated and sweeping rejection of religious language to a suspicion of 'all' language.

I attempted to deal with this problematic in Part 1. Religious, scientific, and ordinary language are related to and distinct from each other in God's created world. They are mean-

---

78   See C. G. Bartholomew, 'Unchartered Waters: Philosophy, Theology and the Crisis in Biblical Interpretation,' in: C. G. Bartholomew, C. Greene, K. Möller, eds. *Renewing Biblical Interpretation*. Scripture and Hermeneutics Series, Grand Rapids: Zondervan, 2000, Vol. 1, 1-39.

ingfull in their specific usage contexts, but this is because they are related to one another and the world in a general usage context that encompasses them all. I have argued that a creational perspective of language, being intimately connected to God, the world, and the self, opens up a possibility for a new understanding of 'all' language as both related and distinct on the level of creation. Such an orientation intends to confront any absolute division between language types, without forging a synthesis that dissolves distinction. I would wager, on these grounds, that either-ors do not fit a theory of language, because they do not fit a theory of creation in its high degree of complexity.

This proposal was put forward as a theological realism. As one who embraces such a view, my hope is that this conception creates fecund discussion and moves towards an alternative that goes beyond the powerful residue of positivism, which continues to haunt language theory at the present time. Furthermore, it seems to me that there is an inordinate amount of time spent on language introspection. No doubt investigations of this genre have merit to some degree and they are beneficial, yet if such painstaking elucidation never arrives at working its way out of details and questions of language usage, in order to draw some general conclusions about the whole of life, one is in danger of getting lost in the reticulation of language that is never merely the context or referent for itself.

In addressing the question in Part 2 on reading Scripture in a special way or as any other text, I aimed to move a polarized discussion forward. There are those who overplay a general— philosophical hermeneutics, while there are others who overplay a regional—biblical hermeneutics. If one makes the biblical text too general there is a loss of its distinctness from other texts, if one makes it too special there is a loss of its relatedness to other texts.

A general—philosophical hermeneutics that underplays regional—biblical hermeneutics is to be faulted for its comprehensiveness, which has the tendency to envelop Scripture within the context of all other books. While it is true the Bible is a text, it is a text unlike any other.

A regional—biblical hermeneutics that underplays general—philosophical hermeneutics is culpable for its narrowness, which has the tendency to focus on the Bible as solely a special book that deals with theology. Granted, Scripture is theological, yet it relates to the interpretation of the world, the self, and the whole of life, not just theology.

It seems to me there is room for critique and embrace on both sides once one takes into consideration a possible both-and proposal that respects relation-distinction. The problem resides in assuming an either-or approach on the question where it is not warranted by the biblical text. Clearly, in other cases this type of approach would be entirely acceptable, even obligatory.

In addition, this assumption unwittingly or perhaps otherwise, attempts to resolve too early the tension that exists at a diversity of levels in the hermeneutical process. A diminution of tension on this question, in my opinion, incurs the risk of being reductionistic and therefore entirely excluding one hermeneutical dimension from the other. Scripture, as far as I can tell, itself points beyond itself to resolution, but for the present tension remains. A position of relation-distinction, on such questions, seems to correspond better with Scripture than polarizations.

It is crucial, in the end, to not leave biblical hermeneutics in the text or with the reader, but to view it in motion and relevant to the whole of life. As interpreters begin in and with the world, this too is where biblical hermeneutics must provisionally and in a finite manner reach its summation. This orientation does not intend to ignore readerly transformation, but only to situate it in a context that is always larger than itself. When one's understanding is modified by the explanation of the biblical text, one's new understanding is to be passionately lived out into the world.

3

HISTORY, FICTION, AND BIBLICAL HERMENEUTICS

Introduction

Jean-François Lyotard's volume, *The Postmodern Condition* and its 'incredulity toward metanarratives,' broke open a large fissure of uncertainty in many disciplines.[1] The rising force of such postmodern ideas is having a profound impact on the discipline of history. In recent years debate among historians has taken new directions. At present, serious challenges pertaining to the truth of written history and the knowledge of the historian are in evidence.[2] While controversy concerning the

---

1   J.-F. Lyotard, *The Postmodern Condition: A Report on Knowledge*, trans; G. Bennington and B. Massumi, Minneapolis: University of Minnesota Press, 1984, xxiv.

2   See K. Jenkins, *Re-Thinking History*, London: Routledge, 1991, 12-32. "We know that such truths are really 'useful fictions' that are in discourse by virtue of power (somebody has to put and keep them there) and power uses the term 'truth' to exercise

truth-value of history has a long tradition, postmodern theories argue for new ways of viewing and doing history. Historical truth, objectivity, facts, events and knowledge are all targets for revision.[3] Marc Trachtenberg expresses his concern in the following manner:

Increasingly the old ideal of historical objectivity is dismissed out of hand. The very notion of 'historical truth' is now often considered hopelessly naïve.[4]

For Trachtenberg, and others, postmodern proposals represent a contemporary crisis in the discipline of history.[5] What is viewed as a radical skepticism and a virulent relativism are considered to be an assault on traditional forms of all that history stands for, including, objectivity, knowledge, clarity and

....

control" (parenthesis his). Also, Jenkins, *The Postmodern History Reader*, London: Routledge, 1997, 1-30, and see the discussion of historiographic metafiction in L. Hutcheon, *A Poetics of Postmodernism: History, Theory, Fiction,* London: Routledge, 1988, 87-120, where it is argued that the problematic we face today is not so much that of a historiographical external reality, but of a loss of faith in our capacity to know that reality.

3   J. Appleby, L. Hunt and M. Jacob, *Telling the Truth about History*, New York: Norton, 1994; B. Southgate, *History: What & Why?* London: Routledge, 1996, have excellent discussions of these matters.

4   M. Trachtenberg, 'The Past Under Seige,' in: *Reconstructing History*, E. Fox-Genovese and E. Lasch-Quinn, eds. New York: Routledge, 1999, 9-11.

5   Zagorin, 'History, the Referent, and Narrative Reflections on Postmodernism Now,' *History and Theory* 38, (1999) 1-24, includes this in a list of several responses by historians to postmodern ideas.

evidence.[6] Facts and truths that are objectively discovered and conveyed were assumed to be the emblem of historical accounts, but this view of history is changing.[7]

The postmodern reply to these assumptions is that new ways of thinking about history are essential. The old Enlightenment fantasies of certainty and objectivity that were thought to be at the center of a writing of history are no longer taken into account. Keith Jenkins states:

.... the attempt to pass off the study of history in the form of the ostensibly disinterested scholarship of academics studying the past objectively and "for its own sake" as "proper" history, is now unsustainable. ...... In fact history appears to be just one more foundationless, positioned expression in a world of foundationless, positioned expressions.[8]

Writing history, for Jenkins and others, is merely a subjective enterprise, exclusively based on literary construction without objective grounding.[9] As such, getting the story straight has little to do with the events of the past.[10] Under the template of

---

6   Ibid., 2. See also, Southgate, *History*, 1-11.
7   Ibid., 5, "In place of grand narratives of this kind, so it is held, have come a multiplicity of discourses and language games, a questioning of the nature of knowledge together with a dissolution of the idea of truth, and problems of legitimacy in many fields."
8   Jenkins, *Postmodern*, 6. (emphasis his).
9   Jenkins, *Re-Thinking*, 12-32.
10   H. Kellner, *Language and Historical Representation: Getting the Story Crooked*, Madison: University of Wisconsin Press, 1989, xi, 3-25, 273-293, argues that as a result of the blurring of distinctions between historiography and literature, we find ourselves

postmodern theory 'new wave'[11] historians argue that a discovery of an accurate recounting of historical events in time is an impossible task.[12] In this scenario, writing history has more to do with inventing meaning, than finding facts. Any pursuit of the truth of historical occurrence in the past becomes highly dubious. How then are we to understand written accounts of past events as 'new wave' historians influence and re-shape the discipline of history? Does the discipline face a growing crisis?

The contemporary debates over history writing and historians also have enormous repercussions for biblical truth, which in some sense, claims to be connected to real events in history. In addition to historical questions, there is another related dimension to our present context that merits consideration. Biblical interpretation is much influenced by the contemporary interest in literary criticism and narrative.[13] The narrative turn has drawn the attention of literary theorists, philosophers, biblical exegetes, theologians and historians, becoming the object

. . . .

needing to get the story crooked. "To get the story crooked is to understand that the straightness of any story is a rhetorical invention and that the invention of stories is the most important part of human self-understanding and self-creation."

11   A. Munslow, *Deconstructing History*, London: Routledge, 1997, 19, refers to "new wave" historians, such as Hayden White and Keith Jenkins, who emphasize the form - content relation and the inescapable relativism of historical understanding.

12   D. Carr, 'Life and the Narrator's Art', in: *Hermeneutics and Deconstruction*, H. J. Silverman and D. Ihde, eds. New York: State University Press of New York, 1985, 108-121, refers to this pejoratively as the "standard" view today.

13   R. Alter, *The Art of Biblical Narrative*, New York: Basic Books, 1981, 15, remarks that a more marked interest in a literary perspective of the Bible begins to arise in the 1970s. See also, H. Blocher, 'Biblical Narrative and Historical Reference,' *Scottish Bulletin of Evangelical Theology* 3, 1989, 102-122.

of intense debate.[14] What is the relation, or lack thereof, between history and historical accounts of the past? How might narratives recount something about the real world? In the light of contemporary literary theories promoted by 'new wave' historians, how are we to view the biblical narratives?

This chapter will reflect on and evaluate recent proposals that are at the heart of these questions. I will focus on three major issues: history and historical discourse; historical discourse and fictional literature; historical discourse, fictional literature and the Bible. My purpose in what follows is to interpret and apply the reflections of the French philosopher Paul Ricoeur to these issues and to draw out several implications for biblical hermeneutics.[15]

---

14   F. Kermode, *A Sense of Ending: Studies in the Theory of Fiction*, Oxford: Oxford University Press, 1966. F. R. Ankersmit and Kellner, eds. *A New Philosophy of History*, London: Reaktion, 1995. H. White, *Metahistory: The Historical Imagination in Nineteenth-Century Europe*, Baltimore: Johns Hopkins University Press, 1973 and The *Content of the Form: Narrative Discourse and Historical Representation*, Baltimore: Johns Hopkins University Press, 1987. S. Chatman, *Story and Discourse: Narrative Structure in Fiction and Film*, Ithaca: Cornell University Press, 1978. P. Ricoeur, *Temps et récit*, 3 tomes, Paris: Seuil, 1983-1985; *Time and Narrative*, trans. K. McLaughlin and D. Pellauer, vols 1-2, and K. Blamey and D. Pellauer, vol 3, Chicago: University of Chicago Press, 1984-1987 and D. Carr, *Time, Narrative, and History*; Bloomington: Indiana University Press, 1986, offer a variety of different perspectives and orientations.

15   Ricoeur's work is one of the most prominent enterprises to peruse for an investigation into the questions of history, narrative and biblical hermeneutics as his writings for the last two decades clearly evidence. Ricoeur, *Temps, I-III*, (*Time, I-III*). 'Philosophies critiques de l'histoire: recherche, explication, écriture,' in: *Philosophical Problems Today 1*; G. Fløistad, ed. Dordrecht: Kluwer, 1994, 139-201; 'Biblical Hermeneutics,' *Semeia* 4, (1975), 29-148; *La Mémoire, L'Histoire, L'Oubli*, Paris: Seuil, 2000. Ricoeur and A. LaCocque, *Penser la Bible*, Paris: Seuil, 1998. (*Thinking Biblically*,

1) History and Historical Discourse

One response to postmodernism and its influence on historical questions has been for some scholars to claim that the text is history. Daniel Marguerat, in a discussion of postmodernism and historiography, argues that there is no history without the written plots and interpretations of the historian. He maintains that any distinction between history and written accounts of history has now been destroyed.[16] A somewhat similar view is advanced by Paul Veyne, who proposes a narrativist model of history that is plot centered; there is no history without the writing of a plot.[17] History, Veyne contends, is made by the written construction of plots.[18]

Such notions of history and writing history are useful in pointing out the role of the historian as interpreter and the importance of narrative configurations, but they have the severe disadvantage of reducing history to interpretation and emplotment, hence devaluing any distinction between historical discourse and history.[19] How do we arrive at historical discourse, a selectively written account of history? There

....

Exegetical and Hermeneutical Studies, trans. D. Pellauer, Chicago: University of Chicago Press, 1998).

16   D. Marguerat, The *First Christian Historian*, *Writing the Acts of the Apostles*, trans. G. J. Laughery, K. McKinney and R. Bauckham, Cambridge: Cambridge University Press, 2002, 5-7.

17   P. Veyne, *Comment on écrit l'histoire*, Paris: Seuil, 1971. Kellner, *Language*, 305-307, esp. 306, has a brief discussion of Veyne's work. He is appreciative of Veyne's position as "it is couched in terms that are *moral* and *aesthetic*." *(Italics his)*.

18   See Ricoeur, *Temps*, I, 239-246 (*Time*, I, 169-174) for a critical interaction with this perspective.

19   I will be using the term historical discourse to refer to written accounts of the past. My hope is that the different terminologies used by myself and others will be clear enough for the reader to

has been much discussion on this issue and it is impossible to cover the wide diversity of views here.[20] I shall closely follow Paul Ricoeur's work and commentary on this controversial aporia.[21] Ricoeur suggests a critical three-fold historiographic operation that comprises, at each level, enrichment and problematization.[22]

First, Ricoeur argues, we begin with an investigation of what we find in sources and documentation. These *detail* sources, for example, traces, testimony, and chronicles can be evaluated and to some degree verified as to their reliability. Sources are not, at this stage, what Ricoeur refers to as 'la connaissance historique' (historical knowledge). According to Ricoeur, on this level, historical occurrence has a twofold epistemological status: it brings about statements of details that can be affirmed or negated by testimony, trace, or documentation, and it plays a role in the overall explanation and narrative configuration, where it passes from the status of a verifiable occurrence to an interpreted occurrence. In spite of the instability of the relation between the occurrence and its documentation there is no

. . . .

discern the meaning of the terms 'history,' 'historiography,' and 'historical discourse,' which all may refer to written accounts.

20   For further discussion see R. J. Evans, *In Defence of History,* London: Granta, 1997. Appleby, Hunt and Jacob, *Telling.* Jenkins, *Re-Thinking.* C. B. McCullagh, *The Truth of History*, London: Routledge, 1998, and Southgate, *History.*

21   Especially, but not exclusively, Ricoeur, 'Philosophies,' 139-201; and *La Mémoire.*

22   Ricoeur, 'Philosophies,' 140, views this enriching as the capacity of one level to bring greater clarity and precision to the other, while at the same time there remains epistemological problems that pertain to each level. Ricoeur, *La Mémoire*, 170, also stresses that the three-fold operation is not to be understood as a chronological succession.

reason to assume that the occurrence was not an *actual* event in the world prior to its documentation.

Second, there is an explicative/comprehension level, which concerns not just 'who', 'where', and 'when', but 'why', 'to what effects', or 'results.'[23] This level comprises such elements as social, political or economic considerations that ripple out from an occurrence in the past. On this level, as Ricoeur points out, there are conflicting models of the *erklären* (explanation) and *verstehen* (understanding) of past occurrences as historical knowledge: some *explain* by subjecting the past to laws or regulations, others *understand* by connecting the past to teleology. The notions of epistemological value are attached to one or the other of these models of cultivating and articulating the past. In effect both attempt, albeit in different ways, to establish something of a scientific dimension of historical discourse through centering on understanding (Dilthey) or explanation (Hempel). However, in Ricoeur's view, the problematic is that explanation without understanding or understanding without explanation results in a truncated epistemology. In the debate between these models, Ricoeur highlights the work of G. H. von Wright in *Explanation and Understanding*[24] (who situates the conflict in Plato and Aristotle). Wright attempts to synthesize the regulatory and the causal or teleological in connection with human action. In finding such a point of view promising, Ricoeur ponders the following question: does a narrative order-

---

23   Ricoeur, *La Mémoire*, 169.
24   G. H. von Wright, *Explanation and Understanding*, Ithaca: Cornell University Press, 1971.

ing assure the unity of a mixed model?[25] This question leads us to the next stage of the historiographic operation.

Third, the interpreted sources and the explanations and understandings are configured in (re) writing a grand historiographical narrative,[26] which aims to be a representation of the past. This (re) writing representation is connected to memory, the intentionality of the historiographer, and the target of recounting truth about the past in dependence on the previous levels. At this point, the historiographical operation is brought to closure.[27] Ricoeur prefers the term 'représentance'[28] for the combined three level operation in order to emphasize that historical representation is working towards bringing to light the targeted reference. These three distinct, yet related levels of operation, offer a critical knowledge of the past.[29]

Ricoeur's threefold notion of the historiographical operation shows that history and historical discourse are not to be equated. For Ricoeur, there is a behind the text or an outside the text that merits consideration in historical inquiry. Trace, testimony, and représentance, stand for something that took place outside the text.[30] While the behind or outside the text are not the only concerns in the interpretation of historical dis-

---

25   Ricoeur, 'Philosophie,' 154.
26   While it is true that there is also non-narrative historiography it is narrative historiography that has recently created the greater amount of discussion.
27   Ricoeur, *La Mémoire*, 169-170, 303-304.
28   Ibid., 304, 340-369.
29   Ibid., *La Mémoire*, 168-169, 323.
30   It is true that what interpreters have is the text, but the text has the capacity to point, beyond itself, to whom and what are behind it.

course, they nevertheless remain valid interests.[31] Historical occurrences only become historical discourse when they are written, while history remains history even though it is not written down.[32] Thus, we are not merely interested in texts, but in a reliable interpretation of the historical character of the events which the texts represent.

2) Historical Discourse and Fictional Literature: The Turn to Literature

The disciplines of literature and modern literary criticism are having a marked impact on the discipline of history.[33] One important reason for this is the contemporary emphasis on literature inaugurated by both French and Anglo-Saxon theorists.[34]

---

31   Ricoeur has stressed that the interpretation of a text is concerned with the world that unfolds in 'front' of the text, but this does not mean that he refuses an appropriate emphasis on a historical referent behind the text. See his discussions in, *From Text to Action*, Evanston: Northwestern University Press, 1991, 75-88; *Interpretation Theory: Discourse and the Surplus of Meaning*, Fort Worth: Texas Christian University Press, 1976; and 'Esquisse de conclusion,' in: X. Léon Dufour, ed. *Exégèse et herméneutique,* Paris: Seuil, 1971, 285-295.

32   D. W. Bebbington, *Patterns in History, A Christian View*, Downers Grove: IVP, 1979, 1-2, points out, "In the English language the word "history" can mean either what people write about time gone by, that is historiography; or else it can mean what people have done and suffered, that is the historical process."

33   See V. P. Long, 'Historiography of the OT,' in: *The Face of OT Studies: A Survey of Contemporary Approaches*, D. W. Baker and B. T. Arnold, eds. Leicester: IVP, 1999, 161-165, for an explanation of the difference between modern and an older styles of literary criticism.

34   Ricoeur, 'Philosophies,' 159, 168-177. Ricoeur discusses these schools of thought, drawing out both the convergences and

The main goals of this section will be to examine Ricoeur's response to new perspectives that attempt to transform historical discourse into fictional literature, and then to map out his own proposals for preserving a distinction.

Louis Mink, frequently understood as a pivotal figure in this discussion was one of the first in recent times to pose the problematic of the relation between historical discourse and fiction. Mink noted that both types of narrative literature 'recount.'[35] His point is well taken, however, it brings with it the following query: if both types of narrative recount is there any difference between a historical and fictional recounting? Mink warns of an impending disaster if the distinction between historical discourse and fiction disappears, although he remains somewhat perplexed as to how one might preserve the contrast.[36] How have postmodern theories in the discipline of history attempted to respond to this problem? This vexing question merits further investigation.

I will now sketch out an analysis of the literary turn in the discipline of history, following Ricoeur's work on two postmodern 'new wave' scholars: Hayden White, and Hans Kellner. White's enterprise has had a profound impact on this

....

divergences in a useful manner.

35   L. O. Mink, *Historical Understanding*, Ithaca: Cornell University Press, 1987.

36   Mink, 'Narrative Form as a Cognitive Instrument,' in: *The History and Narrative Reader*, G. Roberts, ed. London: Routledge, 2001, 211-220. For a fecund discussion of this issue see, M. Sternberg, *The Poetics of Biblical Narrative. Ideological Literature and the Drama of Reading*, Bloomington: Indiana University Press, 1985, 1-57, and Long, *The Art of Biblical History*, Grand Rapids: Zondervan, 1994, esp. 54-87.

discussion, and thus is important to peruse in more detail.[37] He states:

.... there has been a reluctance to consider historical narratives as what they most manifestly are: verbal fictions, the contents of which are as much *invented* as *found* and the forms of which have more in common with their counterparts in literature than they have with those in the sciences.[38]

It is sometimes said that the aim of the historian is to explain the past by "finding", "identifying", or "uncovering", the "stories" that lie buried in chronicles; and that the difference between "history" and "fiction" resides in the fact that the historian "finds" his stories, whereas the fiction writer "invents" his. This conception of the historian's task, however, obscures the extent to which "invention" also plays a part in the historian's operations.[39]

White's complex taxonomy cannot be fully developed here. My purpose in what follows is to briefly uncover something of its trajectory.[40] Two of White's major presuppositions are that the historian invents as much as finds, and that narratives are a

---

37   H. White has sent shock waves through, and had a tremendous influence on, the discipline of history. See R. Jacoby, 'A New Intellectual History?' in: *Reconstructing*, 94-118. Munslow, *Deconstructing*, 140-162.

38   White, 'The Historical Text as a Literary Artifact,' in: *History and Theory*, Oxford: Blackwell, 1998, 15-33, esp. 16. *(Italics his).*

39   White, *Metahistory*, 6-7. For White, in a "chronicle" an event is merely "there," whereas in history writing events are assigned different functions in the story.

40   See Munslow, *Deconstructing*, 140-162 for a fuller introduction to White's views.

mode of recounting, not a mode of discovery.[41] He views the historian as working with disordered and unrelated chronicle type data. The writer then imposes a sequential order, — beginning, middle, end, and an emplotment strategy, which may take the form of a romance - tragedy - comedy - satire. By virtue of this imposition of a form, which is the mode of explanation, moral meaning or content is attached to the narrative.[42] In White's point of view, a plot form or structure functions as a control model, a sort of pre-encoding, a metahistory.[43] This is because emploting presides over and is that through which the historian is obliged to recount the story.

---

41   White, 'Afterword,' in: V. Bonnell, L. Hunt, eds. *Beyond the Cultural Turn*, Berkeley: University of California Press, 1999, 315--324, argues that it is an illusion that "facts" are discovered not constructed. N. Carroll, 'Interpretation, History and Narrative,' in: *The History and Narrative Reader*, G. Roberts, ed. London: Routledge, 2001, 246-265, esp., 251, usefully points out in respect to White's view, "The notion of *invention* here is a bit tricky and open to equivocation. In one sense, historical narratives are inventions, viz. in the sense they are made by historians; but it is not clear that it follows from this that they are *made-up* (and are, therefore, fictional)." (*Italics* and parenthesis his).

42   White, 'Narrativization,' in: *On Narrative*, W. J. T. Mitchell, ed. Chicago: University of Chicago Press, 1981, 249-254, esp. 253, narrativization teaches about "moral wisdom, or rather about the irreducible moralism of a life lived under the conditions of culture rather than nature … . narrative has the power to teach what it means to be *moral* beings (rather than machines endowed with consciousness)." (*Italics* and parenthesis his).

43   White, *Metahistory*. See Kellner, *Language*, 193-227, esp., 197 for a discussion of *Metahistory*. Kellner reads White's worldview as centered on humanism. Historiography is about human choice and a fortification of human mastery, connected to rhetorical language power. Also, W. H. Dray, 'Narrative and Historical Realism,' in: *The History and Narrative*, 157-180, for an insightful discussion of White's views.

White observes:

History-writing thrives on the discovery of all the possible plot structures that might be invoked to endow sets of events with different meanings. And our understanding of the past increases precisely in the degree to which we succeed in determining how far that past conforms to the strategies of sense-making that are contained in their purest forms in literary art.[44]

On the narrative level, the historian constructs narrative meaning through the chosen plot form or typology as a literary endeavor. This literary configuring gives the narrative a fictional content, while a reliable representation of events in the world pales into relative obscurity on the referent register of the grand narrative.[45]

The fact that narratives are constructed is not in dispute, yet there are questions concerning White's views. Why should narrative construction, which many scholars acknowledge, banish historical occurrence, sense and reference? Does narrative construction exclude a credible representation of the past?[46]

---

44   White, 'Historical,' 15-33, esp. 24.

45   White is correct to reject a naïve realism found in a positivist notion of historical discourse, but his reclassification seems to do away with the problematic of the referential dimension of such a literature. See Ricoeur, *La Mémoire*, 324-333.

46   See A. P. Norman, 'Telling it Like it Was,' in: *The History and Narrative*, 181-196, esp., 191, who argues, "A good historian will interact dialogically with the historical record, recognizing the limits it places on possible construals of the past. Of course historians select their facts, and obviously the stories they tell are incomplete. But by itself this does not mean that the result is distorted or false."

Furthermore, why should one presuppose there is no narrative structure (beginning, middle and end), which a narrative may reflect, prior to its literary construction?[47] While appreciative of White's emphasis on the structured imagination and its correlation to creativity and form, Ricoeur remarks:

On the other hand, I deplore the impasse in which H. White encloses himself in treating the operations of emplotment as explicative modes, at best indifferent to the scientific procedures of historical knowledge, at worst a substitute for these. There is a real *category mistake* here which engenders a legitimate suspicion concerning the capacity of this rhetorical theory to draw a strong line between historical narrative and fictional narrative (récit historique et récit de fiction.)[48]

White's theory includes further drawbacks. He both neglects the realist dimension of fiction and stresses an almost exclusive focus on the choice of pre-narrative strategies and emplotment, to the detriment of a concern for the fidelity of a representation

---

47   White, *The Content*, 192-193, strongly argues that there is no narrative structure in life, prior to a literary construction. Carr, *Time*, 49-50, 59-60, esp. 49, maintains that White and other theorists treat structures, "as if they were imposed on meaningless data by the act of narration itself, as if the events of life, experiences and actions, had no structure in themselves and achieved it only at the hand of a literary invention." Carr challenges White's perspective, contending that life itself has inherent structures that are reflected in narrative.

48   Ricoeur, *La Mémoire*, 327-328. (*Italics his*). *La Mémoire* has not, to my knowledge, appeared in English. The English translations for this work are mine.

of the past.[49] One of the marked results of this strategy is that it becomes necessary to view historical discourse as constitutive of, rather than connected to, historical occurrence and life.[50]

Historical investigation and the view of historical discourse today have been strongly influenced by White's work. He has made a forceful contribution to moving historical discourse from the domains of history, literature, science and epistemology, and locating it exclusively in the realm of literature. White relegates or reduces historical inquiry to a third level (in Ricoeur's operation) literary quest.[51] In so doing, White's views render it extremely difficult to draw distinctions between historical discourse and fiction.[52] The major aporia that such an incapacity creates is that it puts in question the reality of the past. Ricoeur states:

... it is the relation between the organizing paradigms of the discipline of history and those which control the composition of literary fictions which has provoked a declassification of history as knowledge with a scientific pretension and its reclassification as literary artifice, and in relation to this caused a weakening of epistemological criteria of differentiation between history proper and the philosophy of history.[53]

---

49   White, *The Content*, 192-196 and 'Historical,' 15-33.

50   W. V. Harris, *Literary Meaning*, London: Macmillian, 1996, esp. 157-174, argues that if historical discourse is merely a narrative construction, fictionality reigns.

51   See the development of Ricoeur's notion of historical discourse above. For Ricoeur, the third level is the last in a sequence which depends on sources (trace, testimony, documents) and explanation and understanding.

52 Ricoeur, *La Mémoire*, 328, notes that it is urgent to "specify" the referential moment which distinguishes historical discourse and fiction.

53   Ricoeur, 'Philosophies,' 171-172. 'Philosophies,' has not, to my knowledge, appeared in English. The English translations for this

Another contemporary scholar who has had a marked influence on the field of history is Hans Kellner. In his work on language and historical representation,[54] Kellner points out that he does not believe there are 'stories' of the past out there waiting to be told or that there is any 'straight' way to write a history.[55] No historical discourse is straight, regardless of the methodological rigor or honesty of the historian. Any historical text, in spite of its straight appearance, is to be understood as rhetorical invention: crooked. Historical epochs or events represented in the text are literary creations that have more to do with self-understanding, than with something that happened in the past. Recounting invented stories, according to Kellner, is how humans understand themselves. There is always a human language story outside the narrative that demands our attention. Getting the story crooked, for Kellner, equally amounts to something of a reading strategy. This means reading a historical text for the areas of concern and decision, no matter to what degree concealed, that have forged particular tactical writing schemes. On his account, underlying rhetorical constructs tell the real story, hence, the need to read stories crooked.

In Kellner's view a rhetorical interest drives historical investigation. Rhetoric and discourse are the other (real) sources of

. . . .

work are my own.

54   Kellner, *Language*. See also, Kellner, 'As Real as it Gets: Ricoeur on Narrativity,' in: *Meanings in Texts and Actions: Questioning Paul Ricoeur*, D. E. Klemm and W. Schweiker, eds. Charlottesville: University Press of Virginia, 1993, 49-66, on Ricoeur and narrative.

55   Kellner, *Language*, 24, 'Historians do not "find" the truths of past events; they create events from a seamless flow, and invent meanings that produce patterns within that flow.'

history, not found in past occurrences or archives.[56] Kellner's presupposition is that historians are lacking knowledge of the reality of the past and that this lack perpetuates anxiety. Historians, as a result, turn from inadequate historical evidence and endeavor to construct the past through language and rhetorical conventions, which attempt to bring order to the potentially terrifying and disordered chaos. On this understanding, rhetoric and language construction are a reality construction. In challenging what he terms, the 'ideology of truth,' Kellner asserts that we are obliged to face the constructed nature of the human world, and to accept that meaning is always reduced to human purpose. Narratives and narrative order constructions are oppressive weapons used by historians in the attempt to mask anxiety and the fear of anarchy concerning the past. Acknowledging a language—rhetorical construction of reality, Kellner argues, amounts to the 'deepest respect for reality'[57] in that

56   Ibid., vii and 1-25, esp. 7, "Crooked readings of historical writings are beginning to abound;..."

57   Ricoeur, 'Philosophies,' 178-179. Kellner, *Language*, 25. In my view, Kellner's work clearly represents a postmodern shift of emphasis in the discipline of history. Historical inquiry into what happened in the past recedes in importance, while literary or ontological concerns (the nature of the historian) flourish. I believe the latter may be the allure of Heidegger's philosophy influencing Kellner. Heidegger's move away from any interest in epistemology to ontology is noticeably marking the disciplines of literature and history. There is no doubt that this change of direction was necessary. In contrast to Heidegger however, Ricoeur attempts to acknowledge the significant import of the turn to ontology, without undermining epistemology. The latter remains a crucial and critical participant in the interpretation of the self, world and texts. See also, Kellner, 'As Real,' in: *Meanings*, 49-66; Ricoeur, 'Existence et herméneutique,' in: *Le*

the reality of the past is merely a product of the historian.

Historical investigation, for Kellner, is not interested in sources, explanations and understandings of historical occurrences in time, but in rhetoric. According to Ricoeur, when the search for rhetoric becomes the sole driving force of the discipline of history, other legitimate historical interests are ignored. If one accepts Kellner's view, truth disappears, and with it, historical reality.[58]

This brief examination of Ricoeur's interaction with two contemporary scholars should not be read as merely a critique of their thought, but also as a means of conveying his own positive proposals. There is a clear indication of how, in Ricoeur's opinion, an over-determined literary focus has the tendency to reduce historical discourse to fictional literature and rhetorical strategies. Ricoeur strongly argues for maintaining the distinction between historical discourse and fictional literature in that historical discourse has different concerns, referents and targets. The reductionism of White and Kellner brings with it an epistemological dilemma with respect to the fidelity of a representation of the past.[59] Ricoeur's conflict with such scholarship has been underscored in showing that the literary—narrative turn, in this school of thought, is now more often concerned

....

conflit des interprétations, Paris: Seuil, 1969, 7-28 ('Existence and Hermeneutics,' in: *The Conflict of Interpretations*, D. Ihde, ed. trans. K. McLaughlin, Evanston: Northwestern University Press, 1974, 3-26,), Laughery, *Living*, 28-42, and Zagorin, 'History,' 1-24, for fuller discussion.

58   Ricoeur, 'Philosophies,' 179.

59   Ricoeur, *La Mémoire*, 170, argues that in the domain of history as a human science, the intentional direction of the historian is to credibly, not completely represent the past.

with literature and literary criticism, than it is with epistemology and scientific inquiry.[60] Ricoeur has forcefully contributed to the move towards narrative as a literary vehicle for recounting events of the past,[61] but he also aims to alert interpreters to the perils of a declassification of historical discourse into fictional literature and appeals for a vigilant epistemology.[62] Historical discourse is indeed literature, yet in Ricoeur's view, it is essential that we not abandon scientific investigation or critical analysis with respect to sources, explanations, and understandings, that pertain to questions of the past.[63]

In addition to the value of Ricoeur's proposals and his critique of White and Kellner, it is important to elucidate further something of his response to the aporetic character of *representation* of the past and then to reflect on his views regarding the problem of distinguishing historical discourse and fictional literature. Several of his personal reflections give rise to thought. Ricoeur affirms the spontaneous realism[64] of the historian implicated by what he refers to as 'l'intentionnalité de la conscience historique' (the intentionality of the historical conscience).

---

60   Ricoeur, 'Philosophies,' 163-168.

61   Ricoeur's work in, *Time and Narrative*, is one major example of this contribution.

62   Ricoeur, *La Mémoire*, 223-226, views a vigilant epistemology as also guarding against a naïve realism, the notion that historical occurrence and historical discourse amount to the same thing.

63   Ricoeur, 'Philosophies,' 167-168. Also, Evans, *In Defence*, 73. See also, Bebbington, *Patterns*, 5, who writes that history is a science in that it is comparable to, "*Wissenschaft*: the systematic quest for ordered knowledge." *(Italics his)*.

64   Ibid., 190. See below. This is a critical as opposed to a naïve realism.

Ricoeur's presupposition here is that,

the historian has for an ultimate object people like us, acting and suffering in circumstances that they have not produced, and with desired and non-desired results. This presupposition links the theory of history and the theory of action.[65]

People of the past are different, yet this difference is not so great that people of the present have no capacity to understand them. The creative connection model here is language, combined with the presupposition that all languages can be translated into our own.

Furthermore, a historian is linked, in a practical, spatio-temporal manner, to the object of study. This schema, chronological in focus though it may be, provides the essential condition of *dating* an historical occurrence.[66] In Ricoeur's perspective the value of this linking goes beyond merely formal chronology. In dating an occurrence the historian is able to connect past actions to calendar time, a mixed time between lived present time and cosmological time.[67] Ricoeur aims to show that historians are indebted to those who came before them and that they receive an inheritance from those of another time. There are others, from the past, who contribute to making us who we are.

A concluding reflection on the aporia of representation of the past is an appeal to trace. Trace is something that someone has left in passing through a place in time.

---

65   Ibid., 191.
66   Ibid., 192.
67   See Ricoeur's extensive discussion of this in *Time and Narrative*.

Ricoeur points out:

Two ideas are involved here: on one hand, the idea that a mark has been left by the passage of some being, on the other, the idea that this mark is the sign 'standing for' ('valant pour') the passage. The significance of the trace combines a relation of causality between the thing marking and the thing marked, and a relation of signification between the mark left and the passage. The trace has the value of effect-sign.[68]

The representation of the past, Ricoeur argues, is not a copy or projection, a correspondence of mental image and something absent, but rather a something represented *standing in place of* that which once was and no longer is. In this sense, the trace does not belong to some form or expression of a naïve realism or idealism, but to what Ricoeur refers to as a 'critical realism' based in a 'profound analysis of what constitutes the intentionality of historical discourse.'[69]

At this juncture, we return to the vexing question that Mink was so instrumental in raising: as historiographical and fictional narratives both recount, is it possible to maintain any distinction between them? In response to this question, Ricoeur has forcefully argued against White and Kellner for this distinction. He appeals to the truth of 'représentance' in that it comprises the expectations, requirements and problems of historical intentionality. A représentance of the past is expected to be connected to reconstructions of actual oc-

---

68   Ricoeur, 'Philosophies,' 196. (emphasis his - parenthesis mine).
69   Ibid., 196. See also, M. C. Lemon, *The Discipline of History and the History of Thought*, London: Routledge, 1995, 4-41, for a fecund discussion of history.

currences, real people, and factual circumstances.[70] This historical narrative articulation can be said to constitute a 'pact' between author and reader.[71] Historians, on this view, are not mere narrators, but argue a case for the actual occurrences and real people they attempt to represent. Historical discourse has a target — a reliable representation of the past. Ricoeur comments:

It is in no way my intention to cancel or to obscure the differences between history and the whole set of fictional narratives in terms of their truth-claims. Documents and archives are the 'sources' of evidence for historical inquiry. Fictional narratives, on the other hand, ignore the burden of providing evidences of that kind.

I should want to stress that as 'fictive' as the historical text may be, its claim is to be a representation of reality. And its way of asserting its claim is to support it by the verificationist procedures proper to history as a science. In other words, history is both a literary artifact and a representation of reality. It is a literary artifact to the extent that, like all literary texts, it tends to assume the status of a self-contained system of symbols. It is a representation of reality to the extent that the world it depicts

---

70   Ricoeur, *Time and Narrative*, III, 142, points out, "Unlike novels, historians' constructions do aim at being *re*constructions of the past ... historians are subject to what once was."

71   Ricoeur, *La Mémoire*, 359-369. See also G. Steiner, *Real Presences*, London: Faber & Faber, 1989, 89-97, who writes of a "semantic trust" without which there would be no history as we know it - a trust between word and world - a necessary covenant between word and object that calls us to respond. He argues for "real presence" versus "real absence."

- which is the 'works world' - is assumed to stand for some actual occurrences in the 'real' world.[72]

In fictional literature, there is equally a 'pact' between author and reader, but there is no expectation, nor demand, for the same level of an extra-linguistic *referent* on the narrative register. While historical discourse and fiction are story, in that both are configured through the imagination and emplotment, historical discourse cannot be reduced to fictional literature. The field of operation for historical discourse is obliged to include other considerations than merely the imagination, plot and a literary form.

As Ricoeur has pointed out, there are major distinctions between historical discourse and fictional literature. First, the goal and expectation of the author and reader are different. Second, historical discourse aims to represent past occurrences in the real world. Furthermore, in historical discourse as opposed to fiction, every effort must be made to work back from the third level grand narrative,[73] to explanation and understanding, to documentation in traces and testimony, in order to critically evaluate the third level narrative claim.[74] Historical discourse claims to represent an actuality behind or outside the text.

---

72   Ricoeur, 'Can Fictional Narratives be True,' *Analecta Husserliana* XIV (1983), 3-19, esp. 4-7.

73   See Section 1 above.

74   Ricoeur, *La Mémoire*, 363. Also, R. Chartier, 'History between Narrative and Knowledge,' in: *One the Edge of the Cliff: History, Language and Practices*, Baltimore: Johns Hopkins University Press, 1997, 26-30.

3) Historical Discourse, Fictional Literature, and the Bible

Postmodern theories have not only had an impact on the disciplines of history and literature, but they are funding much of the discussion in biblical studies, biblical hermeneutics and theology.[75] It has been suggested that theological modernists may be left longing for the nostalgia of presence, while theological postmodernists play with juxtaposition in the absence of sense and referent.[76] George Aichele Jr. states:

Postmodern thought centers upon a fantastic, generic indeterminacy, the non-identity and self-referentiality inherent in language, which makes decisive truth claims impossible. Insofar as one can continue to speak of reality at all, it is generically indeterminate, fantastic.

We never escape from the literal alphabetic surface and its endless dissemination to an ideal, conceptual realm; the fantastic fictionality of language undercuts every attempt to refer to an extratextual reality.[77]

In addition to this form of postmodern skepticism towards a reality outside ourselves and textual reference, the recent flourishing of narrative criticism in literature has contributed to raising a number of questions for the interpretation of the Bible. Does the biblical text have the capacity to have extralingustic refer-

75   S. D. Moore, ' "The Post Age," Stamp,' *Journal of the American Academy of Religion* LVII/3 (1989), 543-559. *Postmodern God. A Theological Reader*, G. Ward, ed. Oxford: Blackwell, 1998. Vanhoozer, *Is There a Meaning?*, are all examples of an awareness of the influence of postmodernism on these fields.

76   G. Aichele Jr., 'Literary Fantasy and Postmodern Theology,' *Journal of the American Academy of Religion* LIX/1 (1991), 323-337.

77   Ibid., esp., 328.

ents? Is there anything 'behind' the text? Do we interpret the Bible as 'historicized fiction' or 'fictionalized history'?[78] There are claims by some that the Bible is fictional in character, while others argue that biblical history and any notion of fiction are in total conflict.[79] My interest in this section is to explore how Ricoeur's views might respond to these questions and forms of postmodern incredulity.

Ricoeur has given us helpful insights in the discussion above concerning history and historical discourse and historical discourse and literature, but precisely how these would now apply to his thinking in the context of biblical hermeneutics must remain somewhat tentative. To my knowledge, Ricoeur has not published on this subject post *La Mémoire, L'Histoire, L'Oubli*, 2000.[80] There are, however, a number of significant earlier

---

78   Alter, *Art*, 1981, 34, 41 uses these terms without a great deal of clarity or identification as to whether they are the same or different modes of narrating. See Long, *Art*, 59-62, for an insightful perspective and clarification of such terminology. Also, Sternberg, *Poetics*, 1-57.

79   See Long's excellent discussion in *Art*, 58-87 of these two views. Long's own position can be summarized in the following manner. The word fiction may be understood in two senses. Fiction is a literary genre and fiction is artistry, creativity, skill. The former may be in conflict with historiography, while the latter need not be. If these two senses are kept in mind, it may be possible to continue to speak of fiction and history as opposites, while at the same time acknowledging that all historiography is fictionalized, while recognising nevertheless that this does not negate the intent to recount historical occurrences in the real world.

80   Ricoeur, post 1994 when 'Philosophies,' was published, has co-written with A. LaCocque *Penser la bible* (*Thinking Biblically*) which appeared in 1998, but this work deals with other relevant matters. To be more precise, a philosopher, Ricoeur, reads the work of an exegete, LaCocque, and comments on it. Ricoeur does not often, in this volume deal with the matters before us.

works that Ricoeur has written which pertain to this, and I will sketch out several trajectories in dialogue with these texts.

While Ricoeur is frequently understood to be affirming different things on the subject of the Bible and biblical interpretation,[81] his general hermeneutical discussion of historical discourse and literature is of value for maintaining that historical accounts have referents outside the text.[82] Working from a general hermeneutical perspective, one must not automatically reduce the biblical text to simply fictional literature. Does this equally hold true for Ricoeur's biblical hermeneutics?

Ricoeur strongly argues for an intertextual approach to the biblical text.[83] This means that biblical narrative must be interpreted in relation to other biblical genres such as wisdom, hymn, prophecy, and so on.[84] Whether it be Exodus, Psalms,

---

81   See, Vanhoozer, *Biblical*; J. Fodor, *Christian Hermeneutics. Paul Ricoeur and the Refiguring of Theology*, Oxford: Oxford University Press, 1995; D. R. Stiver, *Theology After Ricoeur: New Directions in Hermeneutical Theology*, Louisville: Westminster/John Knox, 2001, and Laughery, *Living*, for recent evaluations of Ricoeur's work.

82   Ricoeur, 'Philosophical Hermeneutics and Biblical Hermeneutics,' in: *From Text to Action*, Evanston: Northwestern University Press, 1991, 89-101. Stiver, *Theology*, 123-136, esp., 124 and 'Ricoeur, Speech-Act Theory, and the Gospels as History' in: *After Pentecost: Language and Biblical Interpretation*, C. G. Bartholomew, C. J. D. Greene, and K. Möller, eds. Grand Rapids: Zondervan, 2001, 50-72, argues that Ricoeur's position is "much more historical than some believe," while including the caveat that he is emphasizing that Ricoeur's philosophical views allow for diverse theological appropriations.

83   Ricoeur and LaCocque, *Thinking Biblically*.

84   Ricoeur, 'Naming God,' in: *Figuring the Sacred: Religion, Narrative, and Imagination*, M. I. Wallace, ed. Minneapolis: Fortress, 1995, 217-235 and 'Herméneutique. Les finalités de l'exégèse biblique,' in: *La Bible en philosophie, Approaches contemporaines*, Paris: Cerf, 27-51, esp. 35.

Isaiah, a Gospel, or letter, each text has a temporal dimension and message that needs to be put into a historical, literary, and theological dialogue with the other. This hermeneutical perspective orients the interpreter towards an investigation and evaluation of each text on a case by case basis in order to determine the author's literary act as expressed in the genre of the text.[85]

Several biblical texts, including Exodus and the Gospels, vehemently announce that there is a theological dimension to history. As a listener to that which is recorded in the Scripture,[86] Ricoeur may be open to a view that the God, who is named by the text, does something outside the text, which is now a représentance in the text. Ricoeur observes:

… the naming of God in the resurrection narratives of the New Testament is in accord with the naming of God in the deliverance narratives of the Old Testament: God called Christ from the dead. Here, too, God is designated by the transcendence of the founding events in relation to the ordinary course of history.

In this sense, we must say the naming of God is first of all a moment of narrative confession. God is named in 'the thing' recounted. This is counter to a certain emphasis among theologies of the word that only note word events. To the extent that the narrative genre is primary, God's imprint is in history before being in speech. Speech comes second as it confesses the trace of God in the event.[87]

85   See Long, *Art* and 'Historiography,' in: *The Face of*, 145-175, who has insightful suggestions on the importance of genre and the various methods of investigating the first Testament.
86   Ricoeur, 'Naming,' 217-235, esp., 224.
87   Ibid., 225, (emphasis his).

Ricoeur does not abandon the historical character of the Gospels. The testimony to the Resurrection,[88] for example, requires the historical status: *something happened*, which left a trace, and was recorded in the narratives as an event in time. The Gospel writers' interpretations concern that *which actually happened.*[89]

The witness is a witness to things that have happened. We can think of the case of recording Christian preaching in the categories of the story, as narration about things said and done by Jesus of Nazareth, as proceeding from this intention of binding confession-testimony to narration-testimony.[90]

---

88   Ricoeur, *La Mémoire*, 457-480, shows the devastating result of the death of metanarratives is the metanarrative of death. He argues that for Heidegger the future is under the sign of *being towards death*, and as such the indefinite time of nature and history are subsumed to mortal finitude. In contrast, Ricoeur contends that death is an interruption and proposes *being towards life* as the desire to be (to live) and the power to act, which gives the historian a remembering voice in time. See also, 604-656, where Ricoeur has a detailed discussion of the notions of love, pardon, memory, and gift frequently connected to the two Testaments.

89   Ricoeur, 'Reply to Lewis S. Mudge,' in: *Essays on Biblical Interpretation*, L. S. Mudge, ed. Philadelphia: Fortress, 1980, 43-44. At this juncture, 1979-1980, Ricoeur is wrestling with the question of whether testimony can preserve the connection between sense and referent. It would appear, from his more recent work in *La Mémoire* and 'Philosophies,' the response would be yes. See also Vanhoozer, *Biblical*, 140-141 and 275-289; Fodor, *Christian*, 226-289; Stiver, *Theology*, 123-124 and 188-250; Laughery, *Living*, 105-148 and 151-162 for more extensive development of this question.

90   Ricoeur, 'Towards a Hermeneutic,' *Essays*, 134-135. Confession is central to testimony, but this in not merely a confession of faith, but also of meaning. For Ricoeur, there is the dialectic of meaning and fact and confession and narration.

Numerous testimonies in the biblical text are not merely text, but they represent, stand for, are a trace of God's activity in time in the real world.[91] Ricoeur has argued that the mark or trace of God in history is prior to it being recounted in a narrative.[92] Biblical historical narrative aims to be a representation of what is behind the text. Ricoeur also draws from the prophetic tradition in addition to the gospel narratives for a notion of testimony. Historical occurrences of God's action have taken place and are witnessed to by the prophets. Prophetic moments are connected to historical moments—testimony is bound to confession and narration—in a motion from first Testament prophecy to second Testament Gospel and letter.[93]

Ricoeur points out, for example, that the Christological kerygma is something 'which demands narrative.' In other words, there is something preceding that which is narrativized, something 'behind' or outside the text. Ricoeur appeals to 1 Corinthians 15:3-8, 'that Christ died for our sins according to the Scriptures, that he was buried, that he was raised on the third day according to the Scriptures, and that he appeared to Peter and then to the Twelve,' arguing that the four aorist verbs show a provocation to narration.[94]

---

91   Ricoeur, *La Mémoire*, 366-367. See also, Ricoeur, 'Philosophical,' in: *From Text*, 89-101. There is a coherence here on the level of general and biblical hermeneutics in that both affirm there is a behind or outside the text that must be taken into consideration in its interpretation. For a discussion of Ricoeur's views of the relation between philosophical (general) and biblical hermeneutics, see Laughery, *Living*, 43-55, and 'Language,' above.

92   Ricoeur, 'Toward a Hermeneuitc,' *Essays*, 73-118, esp., 79.

93   Ricoeur, 'Biblical Hermeneutics,' 135-139.

94   Ricoeur, 'Le récit interprétative. Exégèse et théologie dans les récits de la Passion,' *Recherches de science religieuse* 73 (1985), 17-

As I have already mentioned above, Ricoeur is often interpreted in a variety of ways on the question of biblical interpretation. He has explored the aesthetic narrative interests of the fictional dimension of the biblical text; however, he has also maintained an emphasis on the realism of its historical event character.[95] One finds in his work an ongoing challenge to a non-referential literary focus on biblical narrative combined with an illuminating historical interest in a representation of times past in the text.

Conclusion

I am now in a position to conclude my reflections. Ricoeur's work on general and biblical hermeneutics gives useful insights for the issues addressed in this essay. First, in contrast to a postmodern uncertainty pertaining to historical discourse and history, Ricoeur affirms there is a real history outside the text and a scientific and epistemological pretension in writing history. His notion of a critical three-fold historiographic operation is carefully crafted to include a diversity of sources, explanation and understanding and a grand narrative. Historians create and construct historical discourse as a représentance of something that was there in the world. The distinction between a text and a world outside the text is crucial if the discipline of history is to remain concerned with the way it once was.

....

38, esp. 20-21; 'Herméneutique,' 27-51 and 'From Proclamation to Narrative,' *Journal of Religion* LXIV (1984), 501-512.

95   Stiver, *Theology*, 196-219. See also, Vanhoozer, *Biblical*, 282, while not always sharing the view that Ricoeur does enough to distinguish history and fiction states: "Indeed, I have already suggested that Ricoeur's own prescriptions for mediating history and fiction and preserving the realism of the event are a sufficient cure for the occasional lapses in hermeneutic equilibrium."

Second, while Ricoeur has emphasized the literary aspect of historical discourse, he forcefully critiques a postmodern declassification of historical discourse into fictional literature. He maintains a distinction between the two on the grounds of an historical intentionality of representation that targets real people, events, and situations. Historical discourse is marked by the truth of 'représentance' which author and reader expect to be reconstructions of the past. Literary strategies and rhetorical constructs however, which attempt to function as modes of explanation, divert an interest in a knowledge of the truth of the past and are a deficient substitute for critical investigation. Furthermore, Ricoeur underscores the importance of epistemology for historical inquiry. This means that historical discourse does not create the meaning of a past occurrence through a literary endeavor, but that it is concerned with explanation and understanding based on the traces—the marks left in passing— testimonies, and documents, which are connected to a real world outside the discourse. Fictional literature bears no such burden. The discipline of history must remain attuned to the risks of a declassification of its subject matter.

Third, there is a rapport between Ricoeur's general and biblical hermeneutics, in that both argue for a real world outside the text and a distinction between historical discourse and fictional literature. Ricoeur's biblical hermeneutics affirm that the Bible is concerned with historical discourse, which aims at recounting events that actually took place. This orientation points to the credibility of a biblical worldview and a theology of history: God is the Creator and Redeemer, the Great Actor of salvation in history. The drama of creation and God's saving action, make a real world and a real history possible.[96] Traces and testimonies of God's activity in the real world filter into the text as a 'représentance,' a targeted *standing for,* which militates against postmodern theories, and their tendencies to reduce the Bible to a text making history or to fictional literature lacking an extralingusitc referent behind the text. Moreover, an intertextual approach to the Bible may open the way towards the historical, theological and literary features of the message of each text in time. The variety of genres in the biblical text have the capacity to point to the living God behind the text. History, as a discipline with scientific, epistemological and literary pretensions must be aware of the problems of reductionism and be open to a consideration of theological insights that offer explanations and new understandings of the real world.

96   See D. K. Naugle, *Worldview: The History of A Concept*, Grand Rapids: Eerdmans, 2002, for a thorough investigation into the subject. A biblical worldview affirms that there is a real world that is related to and distinct from the human constructions and productions of historical discourse, fiction, or language. How could there be fiction if there was no real world from which to measure and evaluate? In other words, the genre of fiction necessarily presupposes the real. On this register, the literary genre of fiction is parasitic in that it must borrow from what is not its own to exist.

4

AUTHORS,
READERS
AND TEXTS

Introduction

The aim of this chapter is to discuss the debate[1] over authorial intention and reader response[2] to the text, with specific reference to the work of Paul Ricoeur. Ricoeur has had, over the last twenty- five years, a tremendous impact on the problematic of

---

1   This subject has received a tremendous amount of attention in our contemporary context. A few examples: E. D. Hirsch, Jr., *Validity in Interpretation*, New Haven: Yale University Press, 1967. W. Iser, *The Act of Reading: A Theory of Aesthetic Response*, Baltimore: Johns Hopkins University Press, 1978. U. Eco, *The Role of the Reader: Explorations in the Semiotics of Texts*, Bloomington: Indiana University Press, 1979. J. P. Tompkins, ed. *Reader-Response Criticism: From Formalism to Post-Structuralism*, Baltimore: Johns Hopkins, 1980.

2   See E. Freund, *The Return of the Reader: Reader-Response Criticism*, London: Metheun, 1987, 7, who points out that reader-response theory or criticism is a term with manifold representations: the implied reader (Iser), the model reader (Eco), the ideal reader (Culler), the actual reader (Jauss), the informed reader (Fish). My concern is limited to the general theoretical component which considers the flesh and blood reader. I shall not focus, for example, on the dimension of readers in the text per se.

hermeneutics in general and biblical hermeneutics in particular. His writings continue to stimulate interest, raise questions, and give rise to thought, hence, the merit of an analysis of his perspective on authors, readers, and texts.

1) A Brief Overview of the Contemporary Context

Seán Burke suggests that the crisis of post-modernism is a crisis of authorship.[3] Where is the author in the contemporary hermeneutical enterprise?

According to Roland Barthes,

the modern scriptor . . . is not the subject with the book as predicate; there is no other time as that of the enunciation and every text is eternally written here and now . . . For him, on the contrary, the hand cut off from any voice, borne by a pure gesture of inscription (and not of expression) traces a field without origin - or which, at least, has no other origin than language itself, language which ceaselessly calls into question all origins.

Succeeding the Author, the scriptor no longer bears within him passions, humours, feelings, impressions, but rather the immense dictionary from which he draws a writing that can know no halt:

---

3   S. Burke, 'Introduction: Reconstructing the Author,' in: S. Burke, ed. *Authorship: From Plato to the Postmodern*, Edinburgh: Edinburgh University Press, 1995, xv-xxx, esp. xxix. "When we consider that the war on totalities must be a war waged on the transcendental / impersonal subject through whose putative construction totalities emerge, it becomes clear that the great crises of postmodernism are crises of authorship even if they still disdain to announce themselves as such."

life never does more than imitate the book, and the book itself is only a tissue of signs, an imitation that is lost, infinitely deferred. Once the Author is removed, the claim to decipher a text becomes quite futile.[4]

For Barthes, authors are absent. Consequently, the attempt to make sense of texts is pointless. Today, authors seem to be ejected from texts as quickly as passengers might attempt to parachute from a burning airplane. Do authors have rights, aims, and purposes, or are they merely ideological constructions?[5]

The notion of the death of the author raises another query. If authors are mortally wounded, can meaning livingly survive? J. S. Croatto, for example, argues that authors die in the inscribing of their message. This sacrificial "act", as it were, is one in which an author lays down his or her life for the cause.[6] When the author disappears, textual meaning resides in the hands of the reader. The work of Stanley Fish and his famous statement concerning texts: "the reader's response is not to the meaning,

4   R. Barthes, 'The Death of the Author,' in: *Image-Music-Text*, Paris: Seuil, 1977, reprinted in: Burke, Authorship, 125-130, esp. 127-128, (*Italics and* parenthesis *his*). W. V. Harris, *Literary Meaning*, 30-35, argues that Barthes is strong on rhetoric, yet weak on explanation. Harris claims that Barthes assumes and does not argue or demonstrate the death of the author.

5   S. Moore, *Literary Criticism and the Gospels: The Theoretical Challenge*, New Haven: Yale University Press, 1989, 38. Moore clearly sides with the latter. "If he is not simply to be regarded as a historical figure inefficiently managing our scholarly discourse in absentia, from some remote point antecedent and external to it, who or what is he in addition?"

6   J. S. Croatto, *Biblical Hermeneutics: Toward a Theory of Reading as the Production of Meaning*, New York: Orbis, 1987, 16-17.

it is the meaning,"[7] strongly suggests that authorial intention meaning is irrelevant because the only meaning available is created by the reader.

Others argue however, that the new views of the author may due to a contemporary shortsightedness. Authors and their intentions were previously considered, prior to these novel developments, as important for hermeneutics.

Kevin Vanhoozer observes:

...... premodernity and modernity alike shared a similar aim in interpretation: to recover the meaning of the text, understood in terms of the intention of the author. ..... up until fairly recently there was a near consensus on the importance of the author's intention.[8]

Should we be captivated by the new emphasis on the death of the author or embrace the older view that the intention of the author is essential for the retrieval of textual meaning? If we are willing to take Croatto's understanding an "act" further, there might still be a place for the resurrection of the author and his or her intention being valuable for the meaning of texts. If the total focus of meaning is located in the reader reading the text, is there any role for the author in the hermeneutical trajectory?

---

7   S. Fish, *Is There a Text in this Class?, The Authority of Interpretive Communities*, Cambridge, Mass: Harvard University Press, 1980, 3.
8   K. Vanhoozer, *Is There A Meaning in This Text?, The Bible, The Reader, and the Morality of Literary Knowledge*, Grand Rapids: Zondervan, 1998, 74.

It would appear, considering the recent proclamation of the authority of the reader, that the answer is no. In both literary theory and biblical interpretation[9] the reader, by decree, requisitions the primary place and becomes the ultimate determiner of textual meaning and viable interpretation.[10] This scenario has led to the reader achieving something of a celebrity standing within hermeneutics.

Susan Suleiman states:

The words *reader* and *audience*, once relegated to the status of the unproblematic and obvious, have acceded to a starring role.

Today, one rarely picks up a literary journal on either side of the Atlantic without finding articles (and often a whole special issue) devoted to the performance of reading, the role of feeling, the variability of individual response, the confrontation, transaction or interrogation between texts and readers, the nature and limits of interpretation - questions whose very formulation depends on a new awareness of the audience as an entity indissociable from the notion of artistic texts.[11]

---

9   S. Moore, *Literary Criticism*, 107. Moore argues, "reader theory in literary studies is a Pandora's box into which we, infant literary critics of the Bible, have barely begun to peer."

10   For some of the implications with regard to biblical texts see, N. Petersen, 'The Reader in the Gospel,' *Neotestamentica* 18, (1984), 38-51. E. V. McKnight, *The Bible and the Reader: An Introduction to Literary Criticism*, Philadelphia: Fortress, 1985. R. M. Fowler, *Let the Reader Understand. Reader Response Criticism and the Gospel of Mark*, Minneapolis: Fortress, 1991.

11   S. R. Suleiman, 'Introduction: Varieties of Audience-Orientated Criticism,' in: S. R. Suleiman and I. Crosman, eds. *The*

What then are we to make of the role of authors and the relatively recent emphasis on readers in response to the text?[12] How is it possible for texts, for example the biblical texts— narratives, to refigure readers lives without authors? Have God and Author been sacrificed on the altar of the reader? Do authors count? If so, to what end?

2) Reading Ricoeur

My primary focus, after having briefly sketched something of the wider context of the discussion in the previous section, is with an investigation into Ricoeur's views on authors, readers, and texts. I must point out, however, that my analysis is not so much centered on the textual landscape of sense and reference (although this remains a consideration), as it is on the general question of how Ricoeur envisions the authors and readers of narratives—texts.

To begin, I shall first undertake an examination of reading and readers. According to Ricoeur, hermeneutics is concerned with more than just the text. Situated within the task of hermeneutics, as opposed to semiotics, both author and reader have a legitimate place and must be included in the operational trajectory of the interpretation of the text.[13]

. . . .

Reader in the Text: Essays on Audience and Interpretation, Princeton: Princeton University Press, 1980, 3-45, esp. 3-4. (*Italics hers*).

12   R. A. Reese, *Writing Jude: The Reader, the Text, and the Author*, Sheffield: Unpublished PhD Thesis, 1995, 3. She states, "I am not interested in discovering *the* meaning of the text. Instead, I want to see the text expand its meaning potential as it interacts (through me) with other texts in the textual sea."

13   We shall see more clearly what role Ricoeur attributes to "author" and "reader" below.

That is, in Ricoeur's narrative vocabulary, mimesis II (configuration) must be connected to the two sides of mimesis I (prefiguration) and mimesis III (refiguration)[14] through the act of reading. Ricoeur points out the following with regard to hermeneutics:

It does not confine itself to setting mimesis II between mimesis I and mimesis III. It wants to characterize mimesis II by its mediating function. …. The reader is that operater par excellence who takes up through doing something the act of reading the unity of the traversal from mimesis I to mimesis III by the way of mimesis II. [15]

In this hermeneutical scenario, the passage from mimesis II to mimesis III takes place through the act of reading.[16] Ricoeur appeals to Roman Ingarden, Wolfgang Iser, and Hans Robert Jauss for a theory of reading a text.[17] Such a theory neverthe-

---

14   For a full explanation of this Ricoeurian terminology and its significance for authors, readers and texts than it is possible to develop here, see Ricoeur, *Temps et récit, I-III*, Paris: Seuil, 1983-1985. (*Time and Narrative, I-III*, Chicago: University of Chicago Press, 1984-1988).

15   Ricoeur, *Temps et récit*, I, 86. (*Time and Narrative*, I, 53).

16   Ricoeur, *Temps et récit, III*, 246-247. (*Time and Narrative, III*, 168-169), argues with respect to the act of reading, that there is a triple dialectic in a phenomenology of reading: discordant concordance, lack of determinacy and excess of meaning, familiar and unfamiliar.

17   R. Ingarden, *Das literarische Kunstwerk*, Second Edition, Tubingen: M. Niemeyer, 1961, (*The Literary Work of Art*, Evanston: Northwestern University Press, 1974). W. Iser, *The Act of Reading: A Theory of Aesthetic Response*. H. R. Jauss, *Towards an Aesthetic of Reception*, Minneapolis: University of Minnesota Press, 1982, and *Aesthetic Experience and Literary Hermeneutics*, Minneapolis: University of Minnesota Press, 1982.

less must continue, in his opinion, to be preoccupied with the problematic of the reference of the text.[18]

However, at this juncture, it is imperative to take a detour into a Ricoeurian shift of perspective. Ricoeur, while continuing to use the term "reference" in *Temps et récit, (Time and Narrative)* modifies it with the new term "refiguration." This is the case for at least the following reasons.

In *La métaphore vive, (The Rule of Metaphor)*[19] Ricoeur wrote of metaphorical reference as extralinguistic. In his opinion, such statements have a capacity to refer outside the closed boundaries of language itself. This outlook also holds true for narrative, yet with regard to *Temps et récit,* Ricoeur, states:

I would say today that a connecting link was missing between reference, considered the intention belonging to the metaphorical statement, and hence still to language, and the being-as detected by the latter. This intermediary link is the act of reading. ..... . Now the act of the poet is abolished in the poem uttered. What alone is relevant is the act of the reader who in a certain way makes the metaphor, by grasping the new semantic relevance along with its impertinence in the literal sense.[20]

For Ricoeur, metaphor is not limited to the innovation of meaning, but it extends to the power of the redescription of the real.

---

18   Ricoeur, *Temps et récit, I,* 117-124. (*Time and Narrative, I,* 77-82).
19   Ricoeur, *La métaphore vive,* Paris: Seuil, 1975, 273-324.
(*The Rule of Metaphor,* Toronto: University of Toronto Press, 1977, 216-256).
20   Ricoeur, *The Philosophy of Paul Ricoeur,* L. E. Hahn, ed. Chicago: Open Court, 1995, 29.

Generally speaking, this relates to our being-in-the-world on the level of both language and ontology. In re-working the conception of metaphorical reference, Ricoeur now extends it to narrative, but because of the complications of reference (which is described as to tied to existential logic or analytic philosophy, for example),[21] he underscores:

I came to say that metaphorical and narrative statements, taken in hand by reading, aim at refiguring reality, in the twofold sense of *uncovering* the concealed dimensions of human experience and of *transforming* our vision of the world. ... refiguring seemed to me .... to constitute an active reorganization of our being-in-the-world, performed by the reader following the invitation of the text.[22]

From this point of view, a reader is not just dealing with textual meaning (sense), but also the textual reference transmitted through its meaning (sense). However, what Ricoeur now views as essential to the hermeneutical equation is the reader, who becomes one of the key reasons for his move from *reference* to *refiguration*.

It is only because text and reader each have a world that there can potentially be a confrontation and intersection between the two, which then has the possibility of leading to a refiguration of

21   Ibid., 47. Also, *Temps et récit, III*, 13, "l'herméneutique du << réel >> et de l' << irréel >> sort du cadre assigné par la philosophie analytique à la question de la référence." (The hermeneutic of the "real" and the "unreal" goes beyond the framework assigned by analytic philosophy to the question of reference. *Time and Narrative III*, 6).
22   Ricoeur, *The Philosophy of Paul Ricoeur*, L. E. Hahn, ed. 47. *(Italics his).*

the world of action.[23] In other words, the configured text— narrative has a world and the reader has a world. Refiguration takes place through the effect the plot (configuration) generates on the reader reading (mediation) and acting on this plot in time.[24]

I shall now bring the detour to a close. A reading theory, according to Ricoeur, transfigures the question of reference into one of refiguration, now incorporating the reader and the phenomenon of reading, which were not taken into sufficient consideration in *La métaphore vive.*[25]

A Ricoeurian hermeneutics also attempts to pay the closest attention to the motion of the unfolding of the world of the text in front of itself, while being less concerned with restoring the author's intentions, which lie behind the text.[26] The vis-à-vis of the text is not its author, but its sense and reference; its configured world. A readerly appropriation of a text means to understand oneself in front of the world the text projects.[27]

---

23   See also Petersen, 'The Reader in the Gospel,' *Neotestamentica* 18 (1984), 38-51, esp. 42-43 for another perspective on text, world, and reader.

24   Ricoeur, *Temps et récit, I*, 116-117. (*Time and Narrative, I,* 77).

25 Ricoeur, *Temps et récit, III*, 229-231. (*Time and Narrative, III,* 158-160).

26   Ricoeur, *Temps et récit, I,* 122. (*Time and Narrative, I,* 81). Also, A. Thomasset, *Paul Ricoeur: Une poétique de la morale*, Bibliotheca Ephemeridum Theologicarum Lovaniensium CXXIV, Leuven: Leuven University Press, 1996, 271-272, who also alludes to this motion in Ricoeur's hermeneutics.

27   Ricoeur, 'La fonction herméneutique de la distanciation,' in: *Du texte à l'action*, Paris: Seuil, 1986, 101-117, esp. 116-117. "Ce que finalement je m'approprie, c'est une proposition du monde; celle-ci n'est pas *derrière* le texte, comme le serait une intention cachée, mais *devant* lui, comme ce que l'oeuvre déploie, découvre, révèle." (Ultimately, what I appropriate is a proposed world. The latter is not *behind* the text, as a hidden intention would be, but in front of it, as that which the work unfolds, discovers, reveals. 'The

Without this mediation by the reader, according to Ricoeur, the text cannot refigure human action in time.

Furthermore, with regard to both historical and fictional narrative, the former through reference by traces and the latter through metaphorical reference, there is an interface with human action in time. As a result of this interface, read narratives have the capacity to refigure the temporality of readerly human action.[28]

Ricoeur, in *Temps et récit, (Time and Narrative)* accentuates the role of the reader in the hermeneutical trajectory. His awakening to the necessary mediation of the reader can be understood from the perspective that he has now given recognition, not only to the epistemological criteria of the text—narrative, but also to its ontological criteria.[29] This new apperception came about because the world of the text had previously remained, in his opinion, a world exceeding the text's structure, yet with the result that there was no way of linking it up with the world of the reader.

In my opinion, Ricoeur joins the contemporary hermeneutical movement with its emphasis on the reader. While he practices a type of reader-response theory, his following of Iser and

. . . .

Hermeneutical Function of Distanciation,' in: *From Text to Action*, Evanston, Northwestern University Press, 1991, 75-88, esp. 87-88). (*Italics his*). Also, *Interpretation Theory: Discourse and the Surplus of Meaning*, Fort Worth: Texas Christain University Press, 92-94.

28   Ricoeur, *Temps et récit, III*, 229-263 and 371-374. (*Time and Narrative, III*, 158-179 and 259-261).

29   Ibid., 148-150, esp. 149. (*Time and Narrative, III*, 100-101). Ricoeur points out that both history and fiction affect their readers and both relate to the "réel". Ontological criteria return at this stage of *Temps et récit*, showing that both history and fiction pose a "représentance" ("standing-for"), which has possible positive affects on readers.

Jauss shows that his is of a milder form than that of Fish or Barthes. However, Ricoeur leaves us with several questions here. What prohibitions are there for readers not to simply devise and be responsible for creating their own meaning/s of the text—narrative? Do readers determine, constitute, or discover textual meaning/s?[30] Is it possible for a reader to misinterpret a text?

I shall now turn to the question of author's intent. Whether a more recent phenomenon or having its origin in a previous era, an "anti-authorial" project has recently constituted itself as a prominent component within the interpretive landscape.[31]

Ricoeur affirms that texts always have authors, while at the same time he argues that texts are to be understood as having an autonomy at the level of the original author's intention. That is, authors continue to be important for texts, but their intentions lose any real authority. Ricoeur points out:

… writing renders the text autonomous with respect to the intention of the author. What the text signifies no longer coincides with what the author meant; henceforth, textual meaning and psychological meaning have different destinies.[32]

30   See N. Wolterstorff, *Divine Discourse, Philosophical Reflections on the claim that God speaks*, Cambridge: Cambridge University Press, 1995, 130-152, for a discussion Ricoeur's view of text and author.

31   For a fuller discussion see, S. Burke, 'Introduction: Reconstructing the Author,' in: S. Burke, ed. *Authorship: From Plato to the Postmodern*, xv- xxx.

32   Ricoeur, 'The Hermeneutical Function of Distanciation,' cited from, *Hermeneutics and the Human Sciences*, 131-144, esp. 139. While this may or may not be the case, Ricoeur shows his assumption

The text's career escapes the finite horizon lived by its author. What the text means now matters more that what the author meant when he wrote it.[33]

For Ricoeur, a text or narrative has an author, but this author's intent is neither retrievable, nor is it significant for its reader. In regard to Ricoeur's understanding of a text as discourse fixed by writing and as event and meaning, it is the event which disappears along with the author's intent, yet the meaning remains fixed by the text. Thus, the author saying vanishes (event) and the said endures (meaning). Ricoeur attempts to preserve the "said," while eschewing what he presumes is a psychological event which is related to the intent of an author.

In the 1998 collaborative volume *Penser la Bible (Thinking Biblically)*,[34] one of Ricoeur's more recent efforts and co-written with A. LaCocque, he continues to devalue authorial intention as a valid part of the hermeneutical endeavor. The biblical text, it is argued, comprises a "dynamisme textuel" at every level of biblical literature, however, this dynamism has no recourse to an author's intent, but rather is related to the original authors being aware of an incompleteness which asks to be, "re-modeled, re-actualized by the community that is the only agent of these texts."[35]

. . . .

that an author's intention is psychological. Might it not be otherwise?

33   Ricoeur, *Interpretation Theory*, 30.

34   Ricoeur and LaCocque, *Penser la Bible*, Paris: Seuil, 1998. (*Thinking Biblically, Exegetical and Hermeneutical Studies*, trans., D. Pellauer, Chicago: University of Chicago Press, 1998, E.T.).

35   Ibid., 11-12. (*Thinking Biblically*, xiii).

The authors state:

Here, let us simply note that the first effect of reading is to confer an autonomy, an independent existence on a text, which thereby opens it to subsequent developments and subsequent enrichments, all of which affect its very meaning.[36]

Ricoeur and LaCocque frame the biblical text as autonomous and in need of a completion or fulfillment by its reading community.[37] From this point of view, it is argued that the autonomy of the text is related to the author, not the audience.

They contend:

The text exists, in the final analysis, thanks to the community, for the use of the community, with a view to giving shape to the community.[38]

---

36   Ibid., 9. (*Thinking Biblically*, xi).

37   See also Ricoeur, 'Herméneutique et critique des ideologies,' in: E. Castelli, ed. *Démythisation et Idéologie*, Paris: Aubier, 1973, 25-64, reprinted in: *Du texte à l'action*, 333-377, esp. 366. ('Hermeneutics and the Critique of Ideology,' in: *From Text to Action*, 270-307, and in: J. B. Thompson, ed. *Hermeneutics and the Human Sciences*, Cambridge: Cambridge University Press, 1981, 63-100, esp. 91), for a fuller statement on the autonomy of the text.

38   Ricoeur and LaCocque, *Penser la Bible*, 12. (*Thinking Biblically*, xiii). Does the biblical text exist solely because of its community of readers? See D. Stewart, 'Ricoeur on Religious Language,' in: L. E. Hahn, ed. *The Philosophy of Paul Ricoeur*, 423-442, esp., 438, for another point of view. Stewart sets forth the perspective that Ricoeur would affirm that without a historical event there is no "text" to confront a community of readers.

However, it is the text itself that is plurivocal and therefore must be read at several levels. As readers and reading communities have differing interests in the biblical text there will be differing receptions of it. A textual plurivocity, which links up with that of a plurivocal reception, underscores a diversity of reading levels engendered by the same text.

In reference to the Bible and what is identified by these authors as the, "communautés de lecture et interprétation" (communities of reading and interpretation), the hermeneutical circle functions in the following manner: in the interpretation of "Les Écritures" this community interprets itself.[39] What is of import to us here is again the affirmation and emphasis on the text and the place it is given within this discussion of thinking biblically.

If this (hermeneutical) circle is not vicious to the eyes of the faithful belonging to such communities, it is because the founding role attached to the sacred texts and the founded condition of the historical community do not designate interchangeable places. The founding text *teaches*—this is what the word *torah* means. And the community receives instruction.[40]

---

39   See L. Fisher, 'Mediation, Muthos, and the Hermeneutical Circle in Ricoeur's Narrative Theory,' in: M. Joy, ed. *Paul Ricoeur and Narrative: Context and Contestation*, Calgary: University of Calgary Press, 1997, 207-219, for a useful discussion of what, in her opinion, is the crucial importance of the hermeneutical circle in Ricoeur's thought.

40   Ricoeur and LaCocque, *Penser la Bible*, 15. *(Thinking Biblically, xvi-xvii). (Italics theirs).*

While the text and the community of readers remain central and authorial intention continues to be underplayed,[41] the function of the text and the community, in the opinion of Ricoeur and LaCocque, are not the same. The text, in this case the First Testament, takes a priority position in the founded community of readers. In regard to this, on the reader's part, there is then a necessary recognition of an asymmetry between authoritative text and listening reader.

In order to listen to biblical thinking, within this hermeneutical proposal, the reader is obliged to enter the hermeneutical circle. This entry requires, according to these authors, a participation in both imagination and sympathy with the act of adhesion through which a community of readers is founded. It is argued that it is only within this

---

41   Ibid., 9. (*Thinking Biblically*, xi). In relation to the text's autonomy there is the added inference of a renunciation of what these authors refer to as the "caractéristique de l'herméneutique romantique," which seeks to discover the intention of the author. While Ricoeur and LaCocque do not entirely deny the appropriateness of biblical research having a legitimate concern for an author, date, and placing of a biblical text, they do argue: "nous tenons que la signification d'un texte est chaque fois un événement qui naît au point d'intersection entre, d'une part, des contraintes que le texte apporte avec lui et qui tiennent pour une large part à son *Sitz im Leben* et, d'autre part, les attentes différentes d'une série de communautés de lecture et d'interpretation que les auteurs présumés du texte considéré ne pouvaient anticiper." (*Italics theirs*). (We do hold that the meaning of a text is in each instance an event that is born at the intersection between, on the one hand, those constraints that the text bears within itself and that have to do in large part with its *Sitz em Leben* and, on the other hand, the different expectations of a series of communities of reading and interpretation that the presumed authors of the text under consideration could not have anticipated. *Thinking Biblically*, xi).

sharing that there is a possibility of accessing the meaning of these texts.

In summary, Ricoeur's work remains axed on the textual and especially since *La métaphore vive* on the reader. He is concerned to refute the psychological excesses of authorial intent text interpretation, which reduces hermeneutics to seeking a connection with another mind, yet he also opposes the thought that the text is a closed system of signs.

While Ricoeur's position may offer a valid critique to some modernist interpretation theories, in my opinion, it has several weaknesses. When Ricoeur argues that a discourse (text) is "somebody saying something to someone"[42] his tendency is to down-play the knowability of the intent of the "somebody" when it comes to the written text. However, is it not possible to critique a rationalist, structuralist, or Romanticist hermeneutics, criticisms that Ricoeur shares, without resorting to the necessary exclusion of authorial intent?

Furthermore, how does Ricoeur's view square with his own position and intent being able to be communicated through his written discourse when he, for example, seeks to defend his not mixing philosophy and theology or vice-versa?

I hope that my readers will agree that I have gone to such lengths not to mix these genres that I might well be accused of personal inconsistency. All things considered, I am more willing to be the

---

42   Ricoeur, *Interpretation Theory*, 30. With respect to the view of Ricoeur and LaCocque mentioned above I propose the following question: Why would imagination and sympathy not also be necessary readerly components when it comes to someone's acts of reading somebody's intended text?

target of this suspicion than of that of confusionism, mixing crypto-theology on the philosophical plane and crypto-philosophy on the plane of exegesis and theology![43]

I would like to challenge Ricoeur's position on the text as it relates to author's intentions. It is certainly true that the intentionality of an author may not always be transparent, but it nevertheless, in concern for the Other and others, demands an interpreter's attention. In my view, there is at least implicit evidence of the practical necessity of the acceptance of the reality that author's intentions do count more than Ricoeur makes them out to, when it comes to the interpreting of texts. I argue that this is true with regard to Ricoeur's own work, as well as to his perspective of the texts of others.

Ricoeur, as I see it, is not entirely consistent. There are a number of occurrences in his work, at least on the implicit level (if not the explicit), of a different perspective. In *Penser la Bible (Thinking Biblically)*,[44] for example, there seems to have been an effort by each author to write in the context of having read the other author's work and taken it into account:

The exegete first wrote out his contribution, then the philosopher responded to it. Next, they both revised their respective contributions in such a way that the final redaction would yield a book in which each author's work took account of that of the other.[45]

---

43   Ricoeur, *The Philosophy of Paul Ricoeur*, L. E. Hahn, ed. 149.
44   Ricoeur and LaCocque, *Penser la Bible*, (*Thinking Biblically*).
45   Ibid., 7. (*Thinking Biblically*, ix).

In order for such a venture to fulfill its goal, it would seem that the other author's intentions cannot be entirely ignored in the process of working together to produce a single volume.[46] These authors also write of their shared conviction with regard to certain points of view, which they have written about in this particular book.[47] However, in taking these authors contention of the autonomy of the text seriously, one must ask if it is rather the text that has conviction, and not per se the authors?

In another context, Ricoeur writes of the practical articulations related to narrative and how Heidegger's existential analysis in *Being and Time* can play a central role, although this must be framed in certain way. Here, Ricoeur firstly seems to presuppose the understanding of Heidegger's intended existential analysis and then secondly, his own capacity to be able to frame this "sous certaines conditions qui doivent être clairement établies" (under certain conditions that must be clearly established).[48] Ricoeur, at least implicitly, accepts both Heidegger's and his own intentions as authors, and I would surmise their relevance for interpreting *Being and Time* and *Time and Narrative.*

One further example of Ricoeur's, at least implied concession to authorial intention, is found in the context of his discussion of the work of Genette on narrative in *Temps et récit II.*

---

46   I acknowledge that the scenario is different with a living author. However, why should it be presupposed that a once living author's literary act is to be minimized when it comes to reading his/her text?

47   Ricoeur and LaCocque, *Penser la Bible*, 16-17. (*Thinking Biblically*, xvii-xviii).

48   Ricoeur, *Temps et récit, I*, 96. (*Time and Narrative, I*, 60).

Ricoeur writes of the "intention" of Genette, not merely what the text says.[49]

I contend that authorial intention, as well as texts and readers, must be taken into consideration in the hermeneutical enterprise. Generally speaking, it is ironic, how authors often demand the right to defend what they have written in a text, in spite of maintaining that the author's intentions are unrecoverable or even unnecessary.[50]

This is also most noticeable, either when authors are asked what they meant when a reader wants to know if they have understood their work or if they are accused, for example, by a critic of meaning something they never intended. The response is frequently, "I meant to say .... in regard to that argument or that person's position, or I did not mean that and have been misunderstood, as I really meant ..... ."[51]

---

49   Ricoeur, *Temps et récit, II*, 121. "En fait, Genette lui-même se référait au texte fameux de Platon dans << Frontières du récit >>. Mais son intention était alors polémique." (In fact, Genette had himself referred to Plato's famous text in his 'Frontiers of Narrative' 128. His intention then, however, was polemical. *Time and Narrative, II*, 180).

50   A most simple example of this is in copyright laws which recognize the "rights" of authors.

51   See Ricoeur, 'Poetry and Possibility: An Interview with Paul Ricoeur,' in: *The Manhattan Review*, 6-21, reprinted in: M. J. Valdés, ed. *A Ricoeur Reader: Reflection and Imagination*, Toronto: University of Toronto Press, 1991, 448-462, esp. 459-460. I have already mentioned several instances of this ambiguity in Ricoeur's work. Two further examples: First, in a response to the question of the subject and society, Ricoeur argues for a subject who is responsible for his/her words. If this is not the case, we are no longer in a position to speak of freedom and the "rights of man." If this is the case, might it not be appropriate to speak of the "rights" of authorship also? Ricoeur calls for an *"ethic of the word"* and the basic moral duty "that people be responsible

The previous argumentation, it may be said, is based on the possibility of questioning "living authors," but is it not arguable that it may equally apply to authors that are not living except through their texts? No one denies, for example, that the biblical writers have passed from the scene. However, is it not possible that we are left with the author's literary action (not so much now being there—but having been there)? In Ricoeur's terminology, perhaps the question could be addressed to him in this manner: is the text not the "trace" or "testimony" of an author intending something to someone? Does not Ricoeur admit as much in the following statement?

The witness is witness to things that have happened. We can think of the case of recording Christian preaching in the categories of the story, as narration about things said and done by Jesus of Nazareth, as proceeding form this intention of binding confession-testimony to narration-testimony. This conjunction is performed in different ways by the four Evangelists, and we could form a typology on this basis. At one extreme of the range we would have Luke; the other

---

for what they say." (*Italics his*). 'The Creativity of Language,' in: R. Kearney, ed. *Dialogues with Contemporary Continental Thinkers*, 17-36, reprinted in and cited from: *A Ricoeur Reader*, 463-481, esp. 477. In an age with such a profound and certainly correct emphasis on human rights should not the rights of an author also be taken into consideration in the interpretation of the text? Second, Ricoeur comments that, "Thompson is right" concerning the emphasis of the "operative concept of the text" in four of Ricoeur's essays. He goes on to write that ".... this concept had been introduced with the express intention .... ." 'A Response by Paul Ricoeur,' in: J. B. Thompson, ed. *Hermeneutics and the Human Sciences*, 32-40, esp. 37. This seems to imply that there could be a getting it "wrong" and an authorial intent.

John. …. But John, of all the Evangelists, is the herald of testimony par excellence.[52]

Do authors and testimony have an interconnection that readers have a responsibility to pay attention to? Vanhoozer offers a helpful observation in this regard:

….. testimony, of all literary forms, is least welcoming to deconstruction and radical reader-response criticism. For the reader to impose his own meaning or to affirm indeterminate multiple meanings is to deny the very nature of testimony; it is to subject testimony to interpretative violence. Rightly to receive testimony, I shall argue, means to attend to and respect the voice of the author.[53]

Conclusion

I shall conclude this investigation in the following manner. Ricoeur has written above that the world of the text remains latent when not read. If this is the case, using his terminology, is it more appropriate to speak of the world of the text becoming a world "for me" when I read it? Perhaps, it is possible to distinguish be-

---

52   Ricoeur, 'L'herméneutique du témoignage,' *Archivio di Filosofia* 42, (1972), 35-61, reprinted and cited from *Lectures III*, Paris: Seuil, 1994, 107-139, esp. 121-123. ('The Hermeneutics of Testimony,' in: L. S. Mudge, ed. *Essays on Biblical Interpretation*, Philadelphia: Fortress, 119-154, esp. 134-137). One wonders if the author continues to have a voice in testimony?

53   See Vanhoozer, 'The Hermeneutics of I-Witness Testimony: John 21.20-24 and the Death of the "Author",' in: A. Graeme Auld, ed. *Understanding Poets and Prophets: Essays in Honour of George Wishart Anderson*, Sheffield: Journal of Old Testament Studies Press, 1993, 366-387, esp. 367-368, for a fuller critique of modern and post-modern perspectives on the author. This essay can also be found re-printed in Vanhoozer, *First Theology: God, Scripture, and Hermeneutics*, Downers Grove: IVP, 2002.

tween text "world — meaning" and "meaning — world" for me.

Does the latency of the world of the text affect its truly being a world? If a narrative is configured at the level of mimesis II would it, whether or not it is read in its world, still remain a world?[54] Is it not possible for a text to be complete without being dependent on its reader to complete it?[55] For example, is a piece of music a piece of music, if it is never played?[56] Ricoeur's readerly point of view, at this stage, is more aesthetic than rhetorical,[57] and as such it favors a reader's response to the text over a reader's responsibility to the intent of its author.

Several recent exemplary works effectively take the intent of the author in a direction that Ricoeur himself has explored and given careful attention to, but not drawn out the significance of

---

54   Ricoeur, *Temps et récit, III*, 239. (*Time and Narrative, III*, 164). Ricoeur states, "Sans lecteur qui l'accompagne, il n'y a point d'acte configurant à l'oeuvre dans le texte; et sans lecteur qui l'approprie, il n'y a point de monde déployé devant le texte." (Without the reader who accompanies it, there is no configuring act at work in the text; and without the reader to appropriate it, there is no world unfolded before the text. *Time and Narrative, III*, 164).

55   Ricouer, *Du texte à l'action*, 'Qu'est-ce qu'un texte?', 137-159, esp. 159 ".... la lecture est cet acte concret dans lequel s'achève la destinée du texte." (.... reading is the concrete act in which the destiny of the text is fulfilled. *From Text to Action*, 'What is a Text?', 105-124, esp. 124).

56   Ibid., 153, "....la lecture est comme l'exécution d'une partition musicale; elle marque l'effectuation, la venue à l'acte, des possibilities sémantiques du texte." (Reading is like the execution of a musical score; it marks the realization, the enactment, of the semantic possibilities of the text. Ibid., 119).

57   Ricoeur, *Temps et récit, III*, 243-245. (*Time and Narrative, III*, 166-167). See M. Warner, 'The Fourth Gospel's Art of Rational Persuasion,' in: M. Warner, ed. *The Bible as Rhetoric: Studies in Biblical Persuasion and Credibility*, Warwick Studies in Philosophy and Literature, London: Routledge, 1990, 153-177, for a useful discussion of rhetoric.

with reference to the written. That is, intended human action.[58] Rather than equating authorial intention with a purely psychological phenomenon, as Ricoeur often does, this support for authorial intention focuses more forcefully on intention as act.[59]

A text therefore, can and should be considered an author's literary act and thus shown the due respect and care of the interpretive act. As it would be inappropriate, or perhaps even disastrous to ignore a speaker's intention, might not this hold true to some degree at least, with regard to a text in general and to a biblical text in particular?

While it is true that textual interpretation is always mediate, indirect, a task of seeking sense, as opposed to immediate, direct, or a giveness of completed sense, a text is never entirely semantically autonomous.[60] Texts are author intended entities, not necessarily enclosed within the psychological constraints of their author, but opened by a literary act which unfolds a world out into the world, which a reader's world is then able to engage with.

I have argued there is an ambiguity with regard to Ricoeur's

58   See for example, M. Sternberg, *The Poetics of Biblical Narrative: Ideological Literature and the Drama of Reading*, Bloomington: Indiana University Press, 1985. N. Wolterstorff, *Divine Discourse*. Vanhoozer, *Is There A Meaning in This Text?* W. V. Harris, *Interpretive Acts*.

59   Vanhoozer, *Is There A Meaning in This Text?*, 225.

60   M. Sternberg, *The Poetics of Biblical Narrative*, 9-11, argues, "As interpreters of the Bible, our only concern is with 'embodied' or 'objectified' intention .... In my own view, such intention fulfills a crucial role, for communication presupposes a speaker who resorts to certain linguistic and structural tools in order to produce certain effects on the addressee; the discourse accordingly supplies a network of clues to the speaker's intention. The text's autonomy is a long-exploded myth: the text has no meaning, or every kind of meaning, outside the coordinates of discourse that we usually bundle into the term 'context' ."

position on author's intention. Is it warranted, or even appropriate to continue to refer to "the author", while at the same time arguing that "the author's intent" can be depreciated when interpreting a text? Perhaps, in the light of this ambiguity, Ricoeur might have considered a modification of his point of view that an author's intentions are by and large irrelevant to the interpretation of texts.

Reversing the flow of the death of the author and the installation of the reader as the sole determiner of meaning is essential for hermeneutics. The intentions of authors must be considered as pertinent to textual interpretation as it is their communicative actions that set the literary genre and content of the text.[61] A search for the meaning of biblical texts is to be concerned with what authors have accomplished as an action of communication. This perspective therefore, is not a return to a psychological intentionality, which Ricoeur rightly critiques, but a turn to the author's literary act.[62]

---

61   D. Dutton, 'Why Intentionalism Won't Go Away,' in: A. J. Cascardi, ed. *Literature and the Question of Philosophy*, London: Johns Hopkins University Press, 1987, 192-209.

62   In personal discussion and subsequent correspondence, I posed the following question to Ricoeur: "how is it possible, in your hermeneutics, to speak of a necessary love for the Other/other, yet ignore the intention of the author of a text?" Ricoeur agreed that it is important to be sympathetic to authorial intention (here the concern was the Bible) and responded in the following way: "The question is not to deprive the authors from their commitment, but to wonder to what extent the authority of the author on his/her text is part of the meaning." Personal correspondence with Ricoeur, 28 May, 1999.

5

ENGAGING
THE PARABLES
OF JESUS

Introduction

There has been a fair amount of lively discussion on Jesus'
parables over the last twenty-five years. This chapter does not
intend to cover the diversity of views proposed during this period, but has a more modest aim. My goal is to bring a sharper
focus to some of the hermeneutical issues at stake in today's
discussion of Jesus' parables. It is essential, in the light of new
hermeneutical perspectives and arguments, that biblical interpreters and exegetes become more familiar with the dynamics
involved in recent interpretative efforts, which influence the
understanding and interpretation of the parables of Jesus. I intend to develop this in three parts.

First, I introduce the issue of parable interpretation in order to situate it in our contemporary context. Second, I explore the directions of the work of J. D. Crossan. Third, I examine Paul Ricoeur's proposals. I have chosen these two interpreters (not often studied in evangelical contexts) as examples of how Jesus' parables are now being read, and furthermore to show how different hermeneutical orientations lead to diverse theological reflections. Lastly, I conclude with an evaluation.

1) Context

Much modern interpretation of Jesus' parables has been focused on the single idea—general principle theory—that emanated from Aristotle's *Rhetoric* versus his *Poetics*. This view is capably represented by A. Jülicher.[1] In adopting Aristotle's classifications as a model for parable interpretation, Jülicher rejected allegory, insisting that parables have one and only one point of comparison. While it is true that Jülicher brought a number of justifiable critiques to the allegorical method, it remains questionable whether or not he offered a better alternative.[2]

Following the efforts of C. H. Dodd and J. Jeremias[3] and their critiques of Jülicher, we have now arrived at a new stage of parable interpretation. Today, hermeneutical overtures and angles, combined with philosophical modes of

1   A. Jülicher, *Die Gleichnisreden Jesu, 2 Vols.* Tübingen: Mohr, 1910.
2   D. O. Via, Jr. *The Parables: Their Literary and Existential Dimension*, Philadelphia: Fortress, 1967, 2-22.
3   C. H. Dodd, *The Parables of the Kingdom*, London: Nisbet, 1935. J. Jeremias, *The Parables of Jesus*, London: SCM, 1963.

thought have a greater impact on the study of the parables of Jesus. Interpretation theories, such as those represented by Crossan and Ricoeur, have had a marked influence on the understanding of parables, and therefore it is imperative to evaluate their contributions.

2) Crossan's Reading of Jesus' Parables

In the work of J. D. Crossan,[4] one of the most significant commentators of biblical parables over the last three decades,[5] we find an illuminating methodological, literary, and theological analysis. Crossan focuses on a number of questions and issues related to the interpretation of parables. I intend to limit myself, however, to two of his particular concerns: what are the purpose of parables and why are there such different and multiple interpretations of them?[6]

---

4   Crossan refers, in many of his works, to the influences of writers such as Stevens, Yeats, and Pound, philosophers such as Heidegger and Nietzsche, and critics such as Derrida and Barthes. One example of this is found in Crossan's book, *In Parables: The Challenge of the Historical Jesus*, New York: Harper & Row, 1973, 81-82. "Heidegger says: 'Because it thinks Being, thought thinks Nothing.' It is this nothing that is, this Nothing, this Nothingness, that Nietzsche warned about with such terrifying accuracy: 'rather than want nothing, man even wants nothingness.' " The frightening challenge, for Crossan, is to dwell in the dialectic between Being and Nothingness. Crossan states, "We are frightened by the lonely silences within the parables."

5   See F. B. Brown and E. S. Malbon, 'Parabling as a Via Negativa: A Critical Review of the Work of John Dominic Crossan,' *Journal of Religion* 64 (1984), 530-538, esp. 530. "Few can claim to have shed as much new light on any genre of biblical literature as Crossan has on parables."

6   Crossan, 'A Metamodel for Polyvalent Narration,' *Semeia* 9 (1977), 106.

Crossan harkens back to the day when there was the illusion of stability, solutions, and a distinction between the world—reality, and our perception of it.[7] In his view, interpreters now find themselves in a world with no fixed center, hence a world which therefore can be described as something of a labyrinth. Such a labyrinth, Crossan proposes, not only relates to the world in general, but to the play of text interpretation in particular.

Parables, for example, can

be played repeatedly and continuously. Since you cannot interpret absolutely, you can interpret forever.

..... we create the labyrinth ourselves, it has no center, it is infinitely expansible, we create it as play for play, and one can no more consider leaving it than one can envisage leaving one's skin.[8]

In the case of parabolic text interpretation, Crossan takes up what he refers to as the metamodel of play.[9] Play, for him, is characterized as a totality that impinges on all interpretation. This play is not be thought of as played off against something stable or fixed, as if there was some standard or point of reference, but is to be understood as that which defines reality as a whole. Crossan argues that play is revealed in communication through signs and that semiosis (his terminology) is a restrict-

7   Ibid., 107. Crossan argues that reality used to limit and prevent "an immediately dangerous and vertiginous possibility of regressus ad infinitum," but those days are lost forever.
8   Ibid., 139 and 112.
9   Ibid., 113.

ed system of signs that endlessly refer to each other.[10] All referents, therefore, disappear inside signs. There is no question here of a sign to external referent relation, but this is always a sign to sign system that is internally enclosed within itself. In this sense, we can align Crossan, to some degree, with structuralism. However, his views, as I now go on to further establish, are not merely those of an ideological structuralist.[11]

Jesus' parables, according to Crossan, are necessarily a permanence of paradox. Parable, in this sense is related to his metamodel of play as its literary counter-part.[12]

Polyvalent narration, ... that is, a paradox formed into narrative so that it precludes canonical interpretation and becomes a metaphor for the hermeneutical multiplicity it engenders. I would like to retain the term parable for this most profound and disturbing form of story.

There is a small room in Vienna's Schönbrunn Palace walled with mirrors. Locate yourself in the middle and you will see corridors

---

10   Ibid., 117. Crossan gives his readers two options here. He affirms the latter. "Either semiosis is mimetic or it is ludic, it either reflects a reality without it or it creates a reality within it." However, while not focalizing on these options per se, I would want to challenge Crossan on his attempt to offer an 'either – or' option with regards to semiosis in what he has already argued is a metamodel - world of play. Do not either - or's relate to antithesis, rather than to infinite play?

11   Also Brown and Malbon, 'Parabling as a Via Negativa,' 531-533, who argue that Crossan's ideas have undergone a perceptible evolution and one can detect the influences of literary theorists and philosophers who some would classify poststructuralist, deconstructionist.

12   Crossan, 'A Metamodel,' 106.

stretching in all directions as far as the eye can see. ..... the corridors of hermeneutics stretch as far as the imagination can reach.[13]

Those modern interpreters who have argued that Jesus' parables are clear moral messages are mistaken. There is nothing stable in parables. Crossan disputes any particular clarity in the parables and prefers to view Jesus as the greatest satirist and subverter, "a master of paradox, and indeed of double paradox. He who finds the meaning loses it and he who loses it finds it."[14] In Crossan's view, the parables of Jesus are not timeless truths or a defense of a previous proclamation he has made, but they are to be understood as what identifies Jesus' historicity and experience of God, which incorporates everything else within it.[15]

In his first book length venture, Crossan already views parables in intra-linguistic terms.[16] The historical Jesus, on Crossan's account, is to be understood as the language of Jesus and most importantly, the parables themselves.[17] Parables, within this framing, are not potential messages of theological clout, but merely linguistic processes that have a structure, yet are lacking in content and referent.[18]

---

13   Ibid., 140.
14   Ibid., 139.
15   Crossan, *In Parables*, 22, 32-33.
16   Ibid. A parable can never refer to anything outside itself.
17   Ibid., xiii.
18   L. M. Poland, *Literary Criticism and Biblical Hermeneutics: A Critique of Formalist Approaches*, Chico: Scholars, 1985, AAR Academy Series, 111, argues that, "Crossan is more interested in describing how parable becomes metaphor than he is in the parable narrative itself. Crossan focuses on the structure and function, at the expense of the content, of the meanings and

Parables aim to subvert and shatter, while leaving little room for reconstruction in the wake of the debris. According to Crossan, the subversiveness of parables moves readers into the Dark Interval leaving them with insecurity to face "the dark night of story."[19] As parables subvert, they also disorient, shock, and surprise. Jesus' parables then, for Crossan, destroy, overturn, and bring about reversal, but they are unable to disclose anything positive about new understanding in regards to the person of Jesus, the world, the Kingdom of God, or the hearer.[20] Crossan writes:

Parable is an attack on the world, a raid on the articulate.

.... parable will establish the very principle of irreconciliation and non-mediation. Parable establishes the principle of doubt against all security. Like satire, parable as such has no programmatic content. Its function is negative and its creativity is that of via negativa.[21]

. . . .

beliefs embodied in the story. He does not seem to see that the content, as well as the function, of metaphor is also dependent on the concrete situation that the narrative depicts and the auditors recognize."

19   See Crossan's next book, *The Dark Interval. Towards A Theology of Story*, Niles: Argus, 1975, 57-60.

20   Crossan, *In Parables*, 26-27. *Cliffs of Fall: Paradox and Polyvalence in the Parables of Jesus*, New York: Seabury, 1980, 94, where parables are referred to as "metaparables" which results in parable being a perfect mirror, not of the world or the kingdom, but of itself.

21   Crossan, 'The Good Samaritan: Towards a Generic Definition of Parable,' *Semeia* 2 (1974), 82-107, esp. 98, 105.

In commenting on the short parable of Hidden Treasure in Matthew 13:44, Crossan briefly refers to a distinction between rabbinic parables and Jesus' point of view.[22] In rabbinic parables, the actions of selling, buying, and finding follow in sequence. All is done as it should be. However, Jesus reverses the succession, making the movement of actions suspect from a virtuous perspective. Crossan argues that this parable suggests a present opportunity, which remains imprecise. Purchasing the field alludes to a making room for detection, but the undetectable is the substance of all. Thus, the parable is an affirmation of how language is not disclosive, but intentionally subversive and non-referential. Crossan observes:

I will tell you, it says, what the Kingdom of God is like. Watch carefully how, and as I fail to do so and learn that it cannot be done .... the more magnificent my failure, the greater my success.[23]

For Crossan, the answer to why there are multiple and differing interpretations of parables is because parables intend to subvert meaning. His primary focus therefore, remains on the negative. In his world, meaning is harder and harder to come by. Consequently, a lack of total meaning results in no orientation, no normativity, and no predication in the language of Jesus.[24] Concerning the parables of Jesus, Crossan privileges

22   Crossan, *Finding is the First Act: Trouve Folktales and Jesus' Treasure Parables*, Philadelphia: Fortress, 1979, 104-106.
23   Ibid., 120.
24   A. N. Wilder, *The Bible and the Literary Critic*, Minneapolis: Fortress, 1991, 122.

discontinuity over continuity,[25] the negative over the positive, and assumes that parabolic language is arbitrary, plurivalent, with a "void of meaning at its core."[26]

What Crossan is arguing for is that the end result of a search for parabolic meaning culminates in the acknowledgment that there is none. This is because God has unleashed, through Jesus' parables, an unrelenting attack on the very form and content of human language.[27] As a result, language is relativized, deficient of meaning, and lacks extra-linguistic reference. In his view, indeterminacy, or an opaqueness of meaning is paradox, and paradox is entirely negative.[28] Jesus' parables are about negation.

Crossan's hermeneutical orientation therefore is entirely pessimistic. He is driven by his affirmation that since there is no absolute interpretation, one must interpret forever. While the former half of his this orientation may be substantiated, the conclusion drawn from it is assumed, neither argued, nor demonstrated. Thus, what this amounts to is the failure of one ab-

---

25   Ibid., 123. "With respect to Jesus' sayings there must have been some substantial appropriation and continuation of the language of the past and its meaning. I myself see the continuity at the level of denotative symbol and conception which Jesus both exploited and revisioned."

26   Crossan, *Cliffs of Fall*, 9-10.

27   Ibid., 20.

28   See Crossan, 'Stages in Imagination,' in: *The Archaeology of the Imagination*, C. E. Winquist, ed. JAAR Thematic Studies 48/2, Chico: Scholars, 1981, 56, where he argues that "paradox is the highest and final stage of imaginative development." Paradox is defined purely negatively. Also, Brown and Malbon, 'Parabling as a Via Negativa,' 537. "In this (Crossan's) scheme, parable is judged to be of positive value only because it is negative in strategy. He gives priority to subversion" (parenthesis mine).

solute interpretation theory (total meaning) being exchanged for the supposed success of another (no meaning).

The direction of Crossan's hermeneutics is playful suspicion, which results in leaving interpreters of Jesus' parables caught within the webbing of the text, a text which overtly means and refers to nothing. Hermeneutically speaking, it is important to be aware that Crossan not only proposes to interpret the parables of Jesus, but he also wishes to use them as an example of the only way to interpret the world.

After having explored and delineated the landscape of Crossan's hermeneutical orientations and how this concerns the lack of meaning and extra-linguistic reference in Jesus' parables, I now turn to develop Ricoeur's position.

3) Ricoeur's Reading of Jesus' Parables

While Ricoeur was not a theologian, he often ventured into biblical and theological territory. His work on hermeneutics in general and biblical hermeneutics in particular, has been prolific. A notable difference between the hermeneutics of Ricoeur and Crossan will become evident in what follows. The parabolic indeterminacy, argued for by Crossan, can be understood to some degree, at least from Ricoeur's perspective, to be text boundaried. In other words, Jesus' parabolic texts have the capacity to resist a total escape of meaning and extra-linguistic referent, in order to disclose as well as subvert. Ricoeur, like Crossan, practices a hermeneutics of suspicion, but he refuses to stop here. Thus, his openness to a hermeneutics of disclosure is indeed a better fit with Jesus' parables themselves. In addition, there is the possibility that parabolic opaqueness is positive.

For Ricoeur, this means that the failure to arrive at an absolute interpretation of the text may also be understood as an indication of a surplus of meaning, rather than a wholesale negation of it.[29] In contrast to leaving their readers completely in the dark, in the concave of the tumultuous uncertainty that reigns in language and life, Jesus' parables as texts have the capacity to refigure reality and to bring about a transformative new understanding of God, the world, and the self. Furthermore, Ricoeur argues that parabolic polyvalence is not entirely open to a gratuitous free play. Texts, even parabled ones, have interpretations that can be considered more or less probable, in spite of their not being absolute.[30] His affirmation of parabolic sense in the biblical text is to be understood as a manifesto that proclaims that he is unwilling to abandon an original biblical textual sense for either the subterfusion of absolute sense, or non-sense.

Ricoeur works with several parables, but for our purposes I shall focus again on the short parable in Matthew 13:44.[31] For Ricoeur, the parable is full of meaning. The implication that parabolic sense is found in the emplotted drama suggests three critical movements. Set in motion are: 1) finding the treasure 2) selling everything 3) buying the field. In Ricoeur's observation, as this motion percolates through the interpreter's imagination, thoughts, and feelings, there is a discovery that "much

29   Ricoeur, *Interpretation Theory: Discourse and The Surplus of Meaning*, Fort Worth: Texas Christian University Press, 1976, 45-46, 55-57.
30   Ibid., 79.
31   Ricoeur, 'Listening to the Parables,' *Criterion* 13 (1974) 18-22, reprinted in: *The Philosophy of Paul Ricoeur: An Anthology of his Work*, C. E. Reagan and D. Stewart, eds. Boston: Beacon, 1978, 239-245, esp. 240-241.

more" is meant than the parable's normal situational context delivers. Finding is a finding of something, albeit and importantly for Ricoeur, the something found is something given, as opposed to acquired.[32] This expression can comprise a variety of encounters: an encounter of people, an encounter of death, or an encounter of tragic situations, all of which affirm and disclose that our lives are not an achievement of ourselves. These various findings then point in the direction of time and a way of being in time. This mode, in Ricoeur's view, relates to "Event par excellence" in the sense that something happens, and therefore we must be geared to and primed for the newness of the new.[33]

Parabolic sense, Ricoeur argues, is not so much to be found in the Kingdom of God, and what it is compared to, than in what happens in the story. In this case, we may infer that an interpreter is historico-critically informed as to the life setting of the parable, however, at the same time becomes aware that the sense of the parable is not entirely understood only in these various situations (as various situations per se), but rather is parabolically turned towards the relevance of the plot, its dramatic structure, and its denouement, as producing meaning beyond the original context.

Ricoeur thus clearly distances himself from the single idea—general principle theory that emanated from a focus on Aristo-

---

32   This "giveness" is important to note, as Ricoeur, in both his philosophical and biblical writings emphasizes the original giftedness of the "given", in contrast to the aquiring of the "something." 'Listening to the Parables,' 241, *The Philosophy of Paul Ricoeur.*

33   Ricoeur, 'Listening to the Parables,' 241, *The Philosophy of Paul Ricoeur.*

tle's *Rhetoric* versus his *Poetics* (Jülicher), and Crossan's theory, which argues that parabolic texts in and of themselves lack the capacity to mean or refer extra-linguistically.

In continuing through the parable, its meaning-full art is subsequently asseverated in the two further critical movements, which must be linked dialectically to the notion of finding. These two movements; selling and buying, can also be called Reversal and Decision.

Ricoeur remarks:

.... much has been invested in this word "conversion," which means much more than making a new choice, but which implies a shift in the direction of the look, a reversal in the vision, in the imagination, in the heart, before all kinds of good intentions and all kinds of good decisions and good actions. Doing appears as the conclusive act, engendered by the Event (finding) and by the Reversal. First, encountering the Event, then changing one's heart, and then doing accordingly. This succession is full of sense: the Kingdom of God is compared to the chain of these three acts: letting the Event blossom, looking in another direction, and doing with all one's strength in accordance with the new vision.[34]

While the finder—doing, and Reversal and Decision are instructive and "meaning-full" elements in the parable, Ricoeur's hermeneutics of suspicion and revelation are in danger of a theological under-reading of the parabolic Kingdom of God (see below). The point however, at this juncture, is that Ricoeur

34   Ibid., 241.

wants to stress that the parable is full of meaning. While it may shock, negate, and subvert, the parable has the ability to reorient its hearer in a meaning-full direction.

This leads us into the related dimension of Ricoeur's concern, as opposed to Crossan, regarding the status of parables in their capacity to refer. While Ricoeur has strongly argued for this dimension of the biblical text, we must ask how it is to be accounted for in parables. For Crossan, as we have seen, the parables are referent-less, but if Ricoeur argues for a referent, specifically what referent does he have in mind? Parabolic reference in one sense, Ricoeur has argued, is human experience. He states it this way:

Could we not say that a poetic language, such as that of parables, proverbs, and proclamatory sayings, redescribes human reality according to the "qualification" conveyed by the symbol Kingdom of God? This would indicate that the ultimate referent of parabolic (proverbial, proclamatory) language is human experience centered around the *limit-experiences* which would correspond to *the limit-expressions* of religious discourse.

The referent, we could say, of the parable is human experience, conceived as the experience of the whole man and of all men, as it is interpreted in the light of the *mimetic* resources of some realistic *and* extravagant *fictions*, themselves embedded in specific narrative structures.[35]

---

35 Ricoeur, 'Biblical Hermeneutics,' *Semeia* 4 (1975), 34-35. (*Italics his.*)

I agree with Ricoeur that parabolic discourse does refer to human experience and a redescription of human reality. However, I want to question whether this is the referential limit of such discourse. That is, are parabolic referents exclusively existential, or is it conceivable that they also include a theological element? How shall we read Ricoeur? Is it possible that his sensitivity for the meaningful self engenders a potential conflict of referents or a seeming one-dimensionalism in regards to parabolic reference in particular and religious language in general? Some of Ricoeur's interpreters would argue this is indeed the case.[36] In their conception, Ricoeur reduces parabolic referents and religious language to selfhood, or a way of being in the world. While it is true, perhaps, that a thin reading of Ricoeur may gravitate towards such a conclusion, it is nevertheless my opinion that a thicker reading shows his position resists such a critique.

It is important to note, according to Ricoeur, that biblical discourse proposes the referent of a new world, a new birth, the Kingdom of God, and a new covenant. All of these referents have their genesis, neither in the given self, nor in the autonomous me, but in the biblical text.[37] I suggest that Ricoeur goes even further. In my assessment, he rightly affirms that the ref-

---

36   H. Frei, 'The "Literal Reading" of Biblical Narrative in The Christian Tradition: Does It Stretch or Will It Break?,' in: *The Bible and the Narrative Tradition*, F. McConnell, ed. Oxford: Oxford University Press 1986, 36-77, esp. 50; W. C. Placher, 'Paul Ricoeur and Postliberal Theology: A Conflict of Interpretations?,' *Modern Theology* 4 (1988), 35-52, esp. 43; K. Vanhoozer, *Biblical Narrative in the Philosophy of Paul Ricoeur: A Study in hermeneutics and theology*, Cambridge: Cambridge University Press, 1990, 140-141.

37   Ricoeur, 'Philosophy and Religious Language,' *Journal of Religion* 54 (1974), 1, 81.

erent of the biblical text, in addition to human experience and a world, is God. Consequently, it is because God is the referent that there can be a given self in opposition to an autonomous me.[38] If this is the case, then it is possible to refute this critique of Ricoeur. God, as Ricoeur has stated, is the central referent of biblical discourse.

One of the features that constitutes the specificity of biblical discourse is, as we all know, the central place held by the referent "God."[39]

In Ricoeur's point of view, God is the referred to in the solidarity signifying of the multiple literary forms of biblical discourse—narrative, hymn, prophecy, parable, and so on. Parables, for example, in the contrast between their realism and extravagance, and the extraordinary and the ordinary, arrowingly aim in the direction, through the plot and its point, of the "Wholly Other."[40] Therefore, in regard to parables, God is named and referred to through the combination of narrative structure, metaphorical process, and limit expression. This

---

38   This is reminiscent of Ricoeur's well known critique of the self-positing subject.

39   Ricoeur, 'Herméneutique philosophique et herméneutique biblique,' 128, *Du texte à l'action*, Paris: Seuil, 1986. 'Philosophical and Biblical Hermeneutics,' 97, *From Text to Action*, Evanston: Northwestern University Press, 1991.

40   Ricoeur, 'Nommer Dieu,' *Etudes théologiques et religieuses* 52 (1977), 4, 489-508, reprinted in: *Lectures III*, Paris: Seuil, 1994, 281-305, ('Naming God,' reprinted in: Union Seminary Quarterly Review 34 (1979), 4, 215-228, Also, reprinted - cited in: 'Naming God,' *Figuring the Sacred: Religion, Narrative and Imagination*, M. I. Wallace, ed. Minneapolis: Fortress, 1995, 217-235, esp. 229).

works out in the following way: the narrative structure recalls the "original rootedness" of the language of faith in narratives; a metaphorical process "discloses" the poetic character of the language of faith; and limit expression supplies the "matrix" for theological language as this language unites analogy and negation, "God is like...., God is not... ."[41]

I contend, in drawing from this broader panorama of Ricoeur's texts,[42] that it is possible to affirm a threefold biblical referent: firstly, God; secondly, the proposed world of the text; and thirdly, human experience. Thus, human reality can be re-described, as it were, because of the primacy of the first and second of this trinity of referents, which always precedes the third.[43] The fusing correspondence of these referents, however, in no way eliminates their distinction from each other, and as such, they can be understood as, "to the limit," while at the same time, "limited," in their capacity to give a totalizing perspective to that which is beyond "limit."

In my view, Ricoeur's hermeneutics embrace meaning and reference in biblical parables. His parabolic configuration engenders a valid critique of Crossan's hermeneutical theory of non-sense and non-reference. The hermeneutical overtures of Ricoeur credit the parable-story with making textual sense as opposed to non-sense, while liberating it from the constraints

---

41   Ricoeur, 'Naming God,' in: *Figuring the Sacred*, 230.

42   In my opinion, Ricoeur's interlocutors focus too narrowly on his *Semeia* 4 article.

43   This too, from our perspective, stands against those (Frei and others) who argue that Ricoeur's general reigns over his biblical hermeneutic. It is however, not any or every text that refers to God, nor can human experience or reality be redescripted in precisely the same way as the world of the biblical text proposes.

of an enclosed intra-linguistic sign system without external referent, and therefore without the mimetic power of "redescribing" human existence. Ricoeur's efforts lead us far beyond the contours of Crossan's relentlessly negating parabolic scenario and offer a vehement affirmation of a parabolic fullness of sense and extra-linguistic referent.

Conclusion

Crossan's careful research into Jesus' parables is instructive. In picking up on polyvalence, an emphasis on subversion, and the aim of Jesus' parabolic teaching to shock and disorient, Crossan provides useful directions for the interpretation of parables. He has done more than anyone to highlight that Jesus is a master of subversion. Nevertheless, his ultimate conclusions are parabolically unconvincing and theologically insufficient. In my opinion, Crossan is over negatively influenced by a contemporary hermeneutics of suspicion and a metamodel of play that is then too comprehensively read back into Jesus' parables.[44] As a result of this hermeneutical orientation, parables only seem to be able to confirm Crossan's views, rather than to offer any positive resistance to an interpretative paradigm

---

44   Brown and Malbon, 'Parabling as a Via Negativa,' 536 point out, "One experiences a tension between Crossan's expressed concern for interpreting the language of the historical Jesus and his concern for a certain philosophy he is predisposed to ascribe to the 'linguistic' Jesus. To equate reality with language, to locate the metaphoric center of language as a semantic void, to see Jesus' parabling as self-concious, polyvalent linguistic play that reflects its own limits and thereby displays this void - to reason this way is in effect to come dangerously close to making Jesus out to be a first century structuralist/deconstructionist."

that is imposed upon them. His hermeneutics leave interpreters with a "world-view," which finally may be closer to his own, than to that of Jesus.

A further point of difficulty in Crossan's analysis of the parables is his restricted centering on parables themselves. When Jesus' parables are too narrowly focused on there is an increased danger of a reductionistic distortion that tends to ignore the wider context of the stories. Not only do parables as parables militate against Crossan's own totalizing perspective, but when situated in their wider narrative contexts it is unlikely that they so readily support his extreme hermeneutical assessments concerning language, sense, and referent.

Ricoeur's hermeneutic of revelation has the advantage of moving readers closer to the parables of Jesus. His work is to be commended for its affirmation that the parables do mean and refer, although Ricoeur could have greater theological clarity here.

In turning to the theological more precisely now, I would question the sufficiency of Ricoeur's interpretation of Matthew 13:44, especially in regard to the theological component of the Kingdom of God. He is likely, in my opinion, to be correct in his view of the Event as gift, but is this the limit capacity of the symbol: *Kingdom of God*, as used by Jesus?

From a Ricoeurian perspective, the response to this question is to point out that the Gospel says nothing about what the Kingdom of God is, only what it is *like*.[45] Jesus, therefore, is not to be

---

45   Ricoeur, 'Le "Royaume" dans les paraboles de Jesus,' *Etudes théologiques et religieuses* 51 (1976), 15-19, esp. 16. However, Ricoeur does seem to go beyond this in, 'From Proclamation to Narrative,'

understood as a theologian who uses concepts, but as a teacher who taught by images.[46] While this is, in some sense accurate, and I am not entirely against this outlook, it is my contention that Ricoeur could legitimately say more theologically.

I shall explain my position in the following way. The parabolic Kingdom of God, seems indeed to be *like* many things, but is this the case, because it is first of all one symbol, that then in turn, functions at a multiplicity of levels?[47] I believe that it is entirely possible that Jesus is able to use all the parabolic imag-

. . . .

Journal of Religion 64 (1984), 501-512, esp. 508, footnote 14, where he points out the Kingdom of Heaven is "like", says what God does.

46   In my view, Ricoeur is in danger of succumbing to the same reductionistic tendencies he critiques in others. Why not concept and image? Ricoeur's penchant to minimize the significance of concept, in this context, relates to his bias against scientific language as opposed to poetic discourse. However, Ricoeur does, in another context, stress the discourse relevance of the concept and seeking its clarity in aiming to hold understanding and imagination together in the hermeneutical process. See Ricoeur, *La métaphore vive*, Paris: Seuil, 1975, 383, *The Rule of Metaphor*, Toronto: University of Toronto Press, 1977, 303.

47   D. O. Via, Jr., 'The Parable of the Unjust Judge: A Metaphor of the Unrealized Self,' in: *Semiology and Parables*, D. Patte, ed. Pittsburgh: Pickwick, 1976, 26. Via writes of Jesus' narrative parables, as stories of God's reign. Also, R. T. France, 'The Church and the Kingdom of God: Some Hermeneutical Issues,' in: *Biblical Interpretation and the Church: The Problem of Contextualization*, D. A. Carson, ed. Nashville: Nelson, 1985, 38. France convincingly points out that the Jewish background of the phrase, along with the variety of associated linguistic forms and areas of reference in Jesus' teaching, shows that the Kingdom of God does not conform to any single subject sphere and therefore functions as a symbol. The point is, the belief that God is King cannot be restricted, exhausted, or entirely expressed by any one referent. "The phrase serves then not so much to define the subject-area of the statement in which it occurs as to establish the conceptual framework within which that statement is to be understood."

es he does, precisely because the "sense" of the phrase is both conceptual and imagical, related to and invoking a complex constellation of thoughts, feelings, observations, and imaginary processes that God is King: God "does" something and that something is to reign in a myriad of ways.[48] Jesus proclamation of the good news of the Kingdom (Mt. 4:23), and that the Kingdom of Heaven (God) was near (Mt. 4:17), and to an even greater extent that it had arrived in his person, deeds, and miracles, at the very least points to the image—concept that God was King, and that this Kingship was manifesting itself in word, deed, and action (Mt. 12:22-29), which was to be equated with treasure.[49]

Despite this critique and preference for a "saying more" in regard to Ricoeur's view of the Kingdom of God, it is evident that his hermeneutical orientation, in contrast to that of Crossan, argues that Matthew 13:44 is full of meaning (perhaps even more full than he acknowledges) and has extra-linguistic referents. The aim and task of the parable is not merely that of subversion, but also that of disclosure. Since the configured parable is full of meaning and refers, it has the capacity to reveal and to refigure reality, bringing about a new understanding of the Kingdom of God, the world, and the self.

---

48   This surely would have been conceived of, in some fashion, by a good percentage of the opponents of Jesus, to whom many of the parables are performed and addressed.

49   G. E. Ladd, *The Presence of the Future*, Grand Rapids: Eerdmans, 1974, 227-228; and N. Perrin, *Rediscovering the Teaching of Jesus*, New York: Harper & Row, 1967, 76-77.

INDEX

D

Davis, S. T. 9, 13, 15, 68, 73
Derrida, J. 39, 129
Devitt, M. 37, 38, 68, 73
Dilthey, W. 74
Discourse 54-56, 67, 71-77, 80,
    82, 83, 85, 86, 88-90, 92, 93,
    97-99, 103, 113, 117, 124,
    140-142, 146
Distinct 22, 25, 43, 44, 46, 48, 57,
    58, 61-63, 75, 99
Distinction 20, 24, 26, 27, 44-49, 57-
61, 63, 64, 69, 72, 75, 77, 82, 85, 88, 90,
97-99, 130, 134, 143
Dodd, C. H. 68, 73, 128
Drama IX, 98, 137
Dray, W. H. 68, 73, 79
Dutton, D. 68, 73, 125

E

Eco, U. 68, 73, 101
Edwards, M. 33, 68, 73
Empirical 35-38, 40-42
Enlightenment 12, 14, 16, 69
Epistemological 9, 15, 37, 73, 74,
    82, 85, 97, 99, 111
Epistemology 10, 14-16, 74, 82,
    84, 86, 98
Erickson, M. J. 3, 68, 73
Evangelicals 2, 6, 8, 9, 12, 13, 16,
    20, 27, 30
Evans, C. S. VII, 8, 13, 15, 27, 68
Evans, R. J. 73, 86
Evidence 5, 9, 10, 11, 13, 14, 15,
    16, 67, 69, 71, 84, 89, 118
Evidentialist 9, 10, 12
Evil 6, 8, 9

Explain 53, 74, 78, 146
Explanation 40, 41, 47, 54, 58, 60,
    61, 65, 73, 74, 76, 79, 82, 90, 97,
    98, 103, 107

F

Faith I, IX, X, 5, 8, 16, 20, 25, 29,
    47, 50, 54, 55, 62, 68, 95, 143
Fiction 77, 78, 81, 82, 90, 92, 97,
    99, 111
Fictional 71, 77, 79, 80, 81, 85, 86,
    88-90, 92, 93, 97, 98, 99, 111
Fish, S. 68, 73, 101, 103, 104, 112
Fisher, L. 68, 73, 115
Flew, A. G. N. 12, 68, 73
Fodor, J. 33, 39, 54, 68, 73, 93, 95
Foundation 10-12, 15
Foundationalism 11, 15, 21
Fowler, M. 105
France, R. T. 146
Frei, H. 51, 53, 54, 141, 143
Freund, E. 101

G

Ganssle, G. E. 29
Geisler, N. L. 9, 13
Genette, G. 119, 120
Gill, J. H. 38
God I, IX, 1, 2, 4-6, 8-16, 20, 23,
    25, 28-49, 53-63, 91, 93-96, 98,
    99, 106, 112, 122, 132-135,
    137-143, 145-147
Gospels 93-95, 103
Green, G. 21
Gunton, C. 44, 59

R

Ramsey, I. T. 40, 41

Reader XI, 53, 57, 60, 61, 65, 72, 89, 90, 98, 101, 103-117, 120, 122-125

Reader response 101

Readers IX, XI, 61, 101, 102, 105-107, 111-117, 120, 122, 131, 133, 137, 145

Reading X, 21, 24, 47, 51-53, 57, 61-63, 83, 104, 105, 106, 107, 108, 109, 110, 114-117, 119, 123, 139, 141

Realism 5, 16, 18-20, 27, 28, 42, 43, 63, 80, 86, 88, 97, 142

Reality 109

Reduction 35, 41, 45, 48, 64, 85, 99, 145, 146

Reese, R. A. 106

Referent 45, 47, 53, 56, 59, 63, 76, 80, 90, 91, 95, 99, 131, 132, 136, 140-146

Refiguration 107-110

Reformed epistemology 10, 14, 15

Related 24, 26, 28, 43, 44, 46, 48, 57, 58, 61-63, 75, 99, 113

Relation 5, 17, 20, 21, 26, 27, 36, 37, 44, 45, 48, 49, 57-60, 64, 82, 88, 93, 96, 131

Relationship 24, 25, 29, 43, 49, 52-54

Religion 9, 22

Religious language 45

Represent 68, 76, 85, 89, 90, 96

Representation 75, 80, 81, 83, 85, 86, 87, 88, 89, 96, 97, 98

Resurrection 55, 95

Reveal XI, 147

Ricoeur, P. VII, IX, X, 4-6, 21-23, 29, 33, 38-40, 45, 47, 49-57, 60-62, 71, 72-77, 80-90, 92-98, 102, 106-125, 127-129, 136-147

Roberts, G. 77, 79

Russell, B. 12

S

Schaeffer, F. A. 2, 3, 4

Scholarship 31, 38, 43, 50, 69, 85

Science X, 36, 45, 58, 82, 85, 86, 89, 96

Scientific 13, 33, 34-37, 39,-41, 45, 46, 58, 62, 74, 81, 82, 86, 97, 99, 146

Scripture I, IV, IX, X, 30, 31, 34, 37, 38, 41-45, 50-59, 61-64, 94, 122

Scruton, R. 17

Sennett, J. F. 6, 7

Smith, J. K. A. IX, 156

Soskice, J. M. 37, 40-42

Southgate, B. 68, 69, 73

Spirit 25, 53, 57, 58, 59, 60

Sproul, R. C. 9, 10, 13

Steiner, G. 89

Sternberg, M. 77, 92, 124

Stewart, D. 33, 114, 137

Stiver, D. R. 33, 38, 46, 93, 95, 97

Subvert XI, 133, 134, 136, 140

Suleiman, S. R. 105

Swiss L'Abri IX, 4

T

Taylor, M. C. 32

Testimony 15, 73, 75, 82, 90, 95, 96, 121, 122

ENDORSEMENTS

"Living Reflections, written by Gregory J. Laughery the Director of the L'Abri Fellowship in Switzerland, is a worthy contribution to contemporary Christian thought in the tradition of cultural engagement championed by Francis Schaeffer, co-founder (with his wife Edith) of L'Abri. Laughery deals with a number of key issues from contemporary Christian philosophy, hermeneutics, and Biblical scholarship, moving seamlessly from philosophy to theology and back. The book is notable for its engagement with both "continental" and "analytic" philosophy, and also for the good sense and balance the author shows in dealing with a number of contested issues."

C. Stephen Evans, University Professor of Philosophy and Humanities, Baylor University.

"Continuing in the spirit of Francis Schaeffer, but with more careful scholarly acumen, Greg Laughery shows how and why philosophical reflection is important for Christian witness. This is philosophical wisdom in service to the Word."

James K.A. Smith, Professor of Philosophy, Calvin College.

"Living Reflections offers five perceptive essays on religious epistemology and biblical hermeneutics, written by an astute and widely read observer of evangelical scholarship."

Lee Hardy, Professor of Philosophy, Calvin College.

"For those wondering what Francis Schaeffer might say about postmodernity and contemporary disputes over language, philosophy, and interpretation, this collection of essays by a third generation staff member of the Swiss L'Abri may provide the answer. Greg Laughery's book runs the gamut of contemporary hermeneutics, using Paul Ricoeur as his sparring partner in each of its five chapters. Here is no despising of the intellect, but a probing reflection on the nature of Christian thought and biblical interpretation. Schaeffer can rest easy: the community at L'Abri continues to ask the right preliminary questions."

Kevin Vanhoozer, Blanchard Professor of Theology, Wheaton College.

"Living Reflections is an extremely accessible introduction to some key questions facing anyone who wants to interpret Scripture theologically and with reasoned integrity. Greg, the Director of Swiss L'Abri, engages with theological, philosophical and hermeneutical dilemmas that are of the utmost importance for both academy and church. What is more, he makes complex issues into user-friendly discussions for both student and pastor, empowering the reader to grasp their significance for our times. The reader is not only led through the issues of foundationalism, authorial intention, the relation between history and text, the place of language and how to approach the parables of Jesus, but done so with the companionship of Dr Laughery's own mentor, Paul Ricoeur. This is a great introduction to hermeneutics, and to seeing how the thinking of one scholar, Ricoeur, can enhance the reader's appreciation and insight into a myriad of problems."

Graham McFarlane, Senior Lecturer in Systematic Theology, London School of Theology.

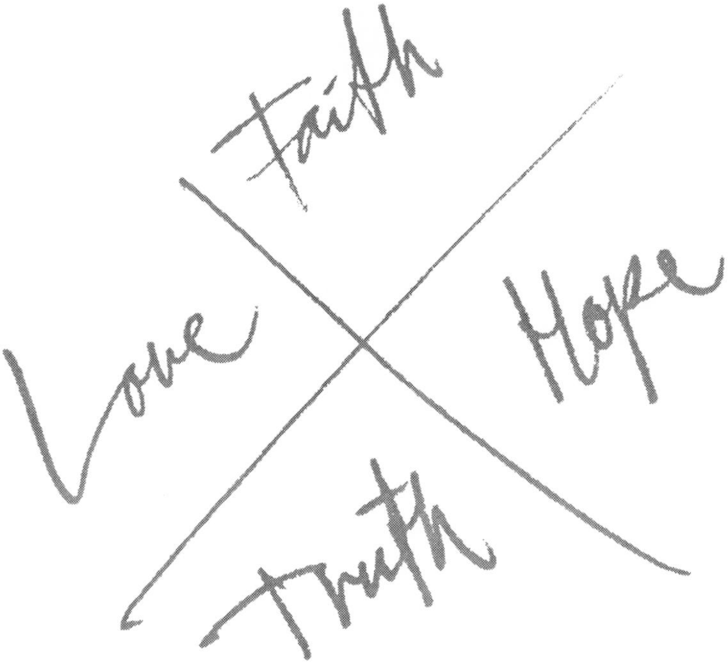
Faith
Love
Hope
Truth

Lightning Source UK Ltd.
Milton Keynes UK
UKOW041914101212

203451UK00002B/83/P